TOTAL HOME SECURITY

How to Safeguard Your Home and Family Against Burglary, Fire and Other Disasters

TOTAL HOME SECURITY

How to Safeguard Your Home and Family Against Burglary, Fire and Other Disasters

by the Editors of

THE FAMILY HANDYMAN Magazine

Butterick Publishing

Library of Congress Cataloging in Publication Data

Main entry under title:

Total home security.

Includes index.

1. Crime prevention. 2. Dwellings–Security measures. 3. Burglary protection. I. The Family handyman.

HV 7431.T67 643 79-621

ISBN 0-88421-085-5

Butterick Publishing
708 Third Avenue
New York, New York 10017
A Division of American Can Company

Manufactured and printed in the United States of America. Published simultaneously in the USA and Canada.

ACKNOWLEDGMENTS

The staff of THE FAMILY HANDYMAN Magazine expresses its appreciation to the many organizations and companies that contributed information to make this book possible, including: International Association of Chiefs of Police; National Sheriff's Association; National Fire Protection Association; General Federation of Women's Clubs; State Farm Insurance Companies; Law Enforcement Standards Laboratory, Institute for Applied Technology, National Bureau of Standards; U.S. Dept. of Commerce; Anoka (MN) County Sheriff's Office; Agricultural Extension Service, University of Minnesota, U.S. Dept. of Agriculture; National Fire Protection Assn.; Lightning Protection Institute; and the Minnesota Safety Council. The book also would not have been possible without the contributions of Gene Schnaser, Gary Branson, Paula Smith, Seph Bloedoorn, Margaret Peiffer, Frank Ivory, Pete Dunham, Arthur Albert, Cpt. Arthur Haggerty, Marian Finney, Richard Bukowski, Paul Swain, Robert E. Armstrong, Richard Bright, Doug Derr, Doug Franklin, Rudolf Graf, Arnold Romney, Tom Philbin, Audrey Singer, Becca Martinson, Keith Wall, Ben Fimon, Candace Casey, Ed Johnson, LoAnn Crepeau and Dawn Johnson.

Howard Jones, *Publisher*

THE FAMILY HANDYMAN Magazine

PHOTO AND ILLUSTRATION CREDITS

By page: 13, Glen Silker; 29, 31, Ron Chamberlain; 36, Emhard Security Products/Ron Chamberlain; 37, Sears; 40, (top) Schlage Lock Co., (bottom) ILCO; 41, Schlage Lock Co.; 42, (top) Medeco, (bottom) New England Lock & Hardware Co.; 43, 45–48, Schlage Lock Co.; 51, Sears; 52, Holmes-Hally Ind.; 54–55, 56–57, Ron Chamberlain; 61–63, Rohm & Haas; 64–65, Seph Bloedoorn; 66, 67, N. P. Steveson/Ron Chamberlain; 69, Rockwell International; 70 (bottom), Arnold Romney; 71, Sanford Corp.; 72, Arnold Romney; 77, BSR/Sears; 79–80, 81 (top), General Electric; 81 (bottom), 82, Duro-Lite; 89, 91, 93–95, Tom Philbin; 97, 98, Ron Chamberlain; 99, 100, First Alert; 101, 102, 103, 104, Ron Chamberlain; 110, Honeywell; 111, U.S. Dep't of Commerce, Nat'l Bureau of Standards/Ron Chamberlain; 112, First Alert; 114, Ansul Co.; 115, Jim D. Brush & Co.; 116 (top), National Fire Protection Association; 117–118, Badger-Powhattan; 119, Bernzomatic Corp.; 122, Sentry; 125, Sears/Ron Chamberlain; 127, Pincor, Generac, McCulloch, Ag-Tronic; 128, Homelite; 129, Rudolf Graf/George Whalen; 131, General Electric; 133, Lightning Protection Institute; 134, Lightning Protection Institute/ Ron Chamberlain; 135, General Electric; 136, Sears; 137–138, University of Minnesota/Ron Chamberlain; 142, 147–148, 149–151, Nutone; 154, ASD; 155, 156 (top), Trine Mfg./Ron Chamberlain; 156 (bottom), 157, Sears; 158–164, Nutone; 169 (from top), Ronson House, Page Alert Systems, Oakridge Industries, W. Roche Co.; 170, The Pine Cone; 171–172, Paul Weissler; 173, Ron Chamberlain; 174, Paul Weissler; 175 (top), Ron Chamberlain; 175 (bottom), 176, Identicar International; 179, Nutone; 183, 184–186, Robert E. Armstrong; 193 (from top), G & G Enterprises, J. T. Hines, Suburban Electronics; 194, Sears/Ron Chamberlain.

Contents

INTRODUCTION 9

1 □ Don't Be a Victim 11

2 □ Watch It, You're Vulnerable! 21

3 □ Strategies to Beat a Thief 27

4 □ How to Lock Doors 35

5 □ What to Do About Windows 53

6 □ How to Mark Possessions 68

7 □ Using Light to Your Advantage 76

8 □ The Canine Approach 88

9 □ Detectors That Smell Trouble 96

10 □ Fire Defense System 108

11 □ Do-It-Yourself Disaster-Proofing 124

12 □ Electronic Alarm Systems 141

13 □ Thief-Proofing Vehicles and Garages 166

14 □ Pointers on Personal Protection 181

APPENDIX: Home-Security Sources 197

INDEX 205

Introduction

■ This book has been compiled with the idea that there are hundreds of ways you can take action to improve the security of your home, once you see how good security measures can be carried out on a do-it-yourself basis. Many involve only a minimal investment in time, money and effort. Most will pay for themselves many times over in reduced injury or property loss, reduced insurance premiums and increased home value. Best of all, the ideas presented on these pages will contribute to your peace of mind, a side benefit for which there is no price tag.

THE FAMILY HANDYMAN'S *Total Home Security* is written for the homeowner and apartment dweller alike, and includes all of the techniques you can use to boost your home security. Few of the suggestions in this book will require more than a modest mechanical ability to put into action. Many don't take even that.

Protecting health, loved ones, home and other property is very much a personal responsibility. However, breakthroughs in understanding burglary patterns, as well as the development of fire protection devices and methods of coping with other disasters have given the modern family more ways to protect itself than ever before—and at a reasonable cost.

The security measures you implement should be tailored to your own situation. Once you've decided security is your problem to handle, the following suggestions will fall into place:

- You can use a variety of low-cost techniques that make your home and possessions a bad risk for criminals.
- You can outwit would-be burglars by beefing up doors and windows with ordinary hand tools and basic do-it-yourself procedures.
- You can take advantage of free community programs designed to help make your neighborhood more secure—for example, Operation Identification and other crime-protection programs.
- You can make effective use of lighting and dogs to add to home security, often without spending more than $100.
- You can install detectors to protect you from fire, gas leaks or storms, at a fraction of what it would have cost only a few years ago.
- You can set up your home with auxiliary power systems which add immeasurably to your safety and comfort during electrical outages, fuel shortages and other large-scale breakdowns.
- You can select from a variety of low-cost equipment that can help thief-proof your car, boat or recreational vehicle and make your garage more secure.
- You can equip yourself both at home and away from home to reduce the risk of being injured or robbed.

Besides doing what you can on your own, you can call on police, fire and safety organizations to help you audit your home's security status. Often conducted by persons specially trained and extensively experienced, their programs can serve as a double check on your work and give you even more ideas on how to make your home more secure.

The threat to home security is real. But so are your opportunities to help control it. Recognizing that you can do something is the first step. We have set out to give you the best information available on do-it-yourself home-security techniques. The rest is up to you.

The Editors
THE FAMILY HANDYMAN Magazine

Don't Be a Victim

CHAPTER 1 ■ You know the fear. How many times have you and your family gone on vacation wondering what you might find when you got back? How many times have you had a sudden flash that the doors weren't all locked, or the babysitter seemed mighty young, or you hoped that the neighbors would be sure to keep an eye on the place and remember to collect the paper and the mail?

How many times have you picked up the newspaper and read about a home burglary, an explosion or fire, and shuddered at how close the address was to your own—or tried to figure how much longer you'll escape the seemingly inevitable violation or destruction of your most cherished of places, your home?

The basis for such fear is all too real. Increases in residential burglary show phenomenal—even explosive—growth. FBI figures show over two million residential burglaries reported annually, with losses averaging between $400 and $500 per incident. Vandalism, another major cause of property loss, has also reached epidemic proportions in residential neighborhoods, and may actually result in greater long-term reduction of overall property values than burglary. Fires in the U.S. claim nearly 9,000 lives each year and injure as many as 300,000 people.

Social factors contribute to the homeowner's concern for security. For example, crimes are often committed by juveniles. Because of their youth, they are much less likely to be deterred by thoughts of some eventual reckoning with a legal system that habitually regards them with the utmost leniency.

Another example: Burglary is a big and successful black-market business supported in large part by otherwise law-abiding citizens who simply can't resist a "steal"—stolen merchandise for sale at outrageously low prices, no questions asked.

Most of these factors are beyond your individual control—you need the cooperation of your friends, neighbors, government leaders and local police. But the physical security of your home can be vastly improved by installing security equipment now being marketed for residential use. Besides cutting your risks, you'll have the peace of mind that comes from knowing you've taken practical steps to protect your family and your property.

MAKING A HOME SURVEY

■ Before you dig into the projects in this book, take a few minutes to case out your home. Check both the interior and exterior. Consider its vulnerability to intruders, fire, explosion, and natural disasters such as storms, lightning, tornadoes and blizzards. Try to think of how a reasonable investment in security equipment could make your home a safer place to live.

You may be inviting burglars by closing drapes, and turning off all lights, radios and TVs when you leave home. Do you "hide" keys under the doormat, or leave the garage door open and unlocked? Are locks flimsy, or do they use keys that have been passed from owner to owner? Is the outside of your home dark at night, surrounded by tall, thick shrubbery that provides good cover for burglars? Do you keep expensive jewelry and important documents at home instead of in a security box? Are valuable items unmarked? Do you leave notes on the door saying when you'll return? When you go on vacation does your lawn grow wild? Do your driveway and garbage cans stand empty? Do mail deliveries stack up?

You may be inviting trouble by overloading circuits and sockets, or using defective appliances and the wrong size fuses. Think about the way you handle matches, lighters and flammables, and whether rags and papers are allowed to pile up. Do family members smoke in bed? Do you have smoke alarms, fire ladders, screens on your chimney, fire extinguishers? Does your family know how to alert the fire department and how to evacuate in case a fire breaks out? Do you know which area of the basement is the safest in case of threatening storms?

HOME-SECURITY COSTS

■ What's the price tag on home security? If you go whole hog with the most sophisticated equipment on the market you'll be spending thousands of dollars. If that sounds like too much, don't give up—you can buy a load of security devices for much less. The tab on top-of-the-line equipment, including deadbolt locks for exterior doors, window locks for first-floor and basement-level windows, plus a safe would fall well short of $1,000. That's a bargain, considering the reduced risk likely to result. Here's a quick glance at the more critical equipment, along with approximate costs, shown in the photo.

1. *Lighting equipment.* Exterior lighting reduces nighttime burglary and vandalism. A mercury lamp with an electric eye for dusk-to-dawn security may run you about $50. A low-voltage outdoor lighting system, for about $80, includes transformer, timer, lamps and cable, and can be installed by a do-it-yourselfer. Timers for interior light control and simulation of normal family routines will generally cost about $10 each.

To make your home secure, consider the items pictured: 1) lighting equipment, including a timer; 2) fire equipment—aluminum escape ladder and fire extinguisher; 3) burglar alarm; 4) locks for windows and doors; 5) gas detector and storm detector; and 6) smoke alarm and fireproof safe.

2. *Fire equipment.* Aluminum escape ladders which fold for easy storage will run about $60 each. They are available in permanently installed types or portable chain designs. Fire extinguishers come in a variety of sizes and fire ratings, and cost somewhere between $6 and $50 each.

3. *Intrusion alarms.* Various hardwired and wireless types are available starting at about $20, with or without central station monitoring. Components bearing the Underwriters Laboratories (UL) seal are recommended.

4. *Window and door locks.* Key locks for windows and deadbolt locks for doors are available in a wide price range. Door locks range from about $3 to $20. Window locks vary from latch types to keyed locking devices, with price tags of 75¢ on up.

5. *Gas and storm alarms.* Gas alarms that detect the presence of natural or propane gas will cost you from about $20 to $60. Storm alarms which differentiate between normal lightning and severe storms and tornado activity are available for about $60.

6. *Smoke alarms and fire-security safes.* Smoke detectors that sound a distinctive signal warning of fire will run from about $12 to $40. A safe that guards valuables and irreplaceable records from fire and intense heat runs from about $150 to $300.

HOMEOWNERS INSURANCE

■ Once you get an idea of the security quotient of your home and the kind of equipment that is needed, take some time out to consider insurance. Homeowners insurance, as it's called in the industry, doesn't make your home more physically secure. It doesn't stop burglars, put out fires, snuff tornadoes or prevent accidents. But it does help you and your family become more financially secure. For a relatively small price, homeowners insurance offers financial protection in the event of most types of misfortune, including potentially expensive liabilities.

Before you take the protective measures described on the following pages, you can back them up with the immense financial resources of a reputable insurance company. A good homeowners or renters policy will contribute to your peace of mind and help fulfill your total responsibility to your family.

Installing specific equipment as shown in this book may qualify you for insurance premium discounts. Many insurance companies offer discounts if you have installed equipment such as smoke, fire or burglar alarms in your home.

Buying homeowners insurance is relatively simple. It's basically a matter of evaluating the company, picking an agent and then working out your specific coverages.

CHOOSING A COMPANY □ Because of the way information about companies is gathered and assembled, it is unlikely you will be able to get completely unbiased recommendations. A good place to start is your state insurance commission or office of consumer protection. Some state governments publish a shopper's guide to insurance companies and many keep records of complaints made against specific firms.

Some of the questions you want to ask include: What's the company's ratio of complaints to premium dollars, compared to industry averages? Has the company been known to engage in arbitrary cancellation, or does it cancel a higher-than-average number of policies on renewal? Have there been numerous complaints about the length of time policyholders have to wait for claims to be paid?

Consumer Reports has featured ratings of nationally known companies based on policyholder experiences. You can check your local library for the appropriate back issues. Also, the media often operate public interest services designed to act as ombudsmen for consumers in trouble. If a newspaper or television or radio station in your area actively assists people in solving problems with business and government agencies, check with them for further information on the company you are considering.

Specific information on the size, financial condition and management of a company is published periodically in Best's *Insurance Reports, Property-Liability.* Like *Consumer Reports*, these guides are probably at your public library. Such guides are tough sledding unless you are of a financial turn of mind, but you can make sure the company you are considering is listed. Best's lists virtually every company licensed to do business in the U.S.

Use your own judgment after you've gone through the information-gathering process with two or three prospective insurers. You may like the idea of signing with a large national company that's been in business for years. On the other hand, a smaller regionally based company with a good record of service may suit you very well.

Your final decision may be based on your experience with the company's agent. He is the key to any successful insurance program. There is no substitute for an honest agent who can advise you competently.

CHOOSING AN AGENT □ One of the best methods of choosing an agent is by asking people you know and trust about their experiences with a specific insurance agent. You may want to ask them the following questions to help evaluate their agent: How long have you had this particular agent? Have you had a claim and were you satisfied with the results? Does the agent or his office staff promptly take care of any changes you request, answer your questions or advise you of ways of updating your policy? Is the agent easily accessible? Does he return your phone call promptly if he is out at the time of your call? Is the agent near your home? Does he come to your home by appointment, day or evening, when it is necessary to get together?

If you cannot find a particular insurance agent through a solid recommendation, there are some indicators to note when you stop at a prospective agent's office. Check the physical location; how well organized the agent and his office seem to be; whether the agent gives the appearance of being successful and established in the business.

You can further evaluate a prospective agent by the way he handles your questions and concerns. A good agent not only answers your questions in a clear and professional manner, but asks questions of you as well. It's part of the process of designing a policy to fit your exact needs. He will offer alternatives, advise you of the availability of additional coverages and offer you a choice of deductibles.

It is most important that you meet your agent face-to-face when you first take out the policy. It gives you an opportunity to personally evaluate the agent and, more important, an opportunity to review the policy, ask questions and get the information first hand. Be sure to avoid the insurance agent who wants to complete the application over the telephone.

To be sure, if you already have an insurance agent who is honest, prompt in service and professional, you already have much of the buying process completed.

BUYING COVERAGE □ Homeowners insurance has come a long way in the last few years, with marked progress made in coverage, service and the issuance of readable policies. The elements of a typical homeowners policy can be broken down as follows.

Dwelling □ This covers the home and any structure attached to it,

HOMEOWNERS POLICY COVERAGES

These coverages apply to certain causes of damage called perils. The perils you're insured against will vary according to the type of homeowners policy you have.

The basic homeowners policy protects you from these important and potentially expensive liabilities:

- *Comprehensive Personal Liability*
- *Medical Payments (other than to insureds)*
- *Physical Damage to Property of Others*
- *All Costs of Defending Suits (whether you are liable or not)*

The basic homeowners policy protects your property from loss caused by these familiar perils:

- *Smoke*
- *Fire*
- *Explosion*
- *Windstorm and Hail*
- *Damage from Non-owned Vehicles*
- *Lightning*
- *Glass Breakage*
- *Riot and Civil Commotion*
- *Theft, on or off Premises*
- *Vandalism and Malicious Mischief*
- *Damage from Aircraft*

You can add to your basic policy to cover these additional perils:

- *Damage from Owned and Non-owned Vehicles*
- *Collapse of Building*
- *Artifically Generated Electrical Current*
- *Freezing of Plumbing System*
- *Tearing or Bulging of Water-Heating Appliances*
- *Weight of Ice and Snow*
- *Water Escape from Plumbing, Heating, Air Conditioning or Appliances*
- *Falling Objects*

Or, you can buy an "all-risk" policy which provides the most comprehensive coverage available. It adds these coverages for your home, plus many others not specifically excluded. These coverages apply only to the building itself:

- *Moisture Damage Caused by Malfunction of Thermostat*
- *Building Damage*
- *Water Damage*
- *Paint Spill*
- *Scorched Surface*
- *Siding Damaged by Missiles*
- *Damage by Wild Animal*
- *Falling Objects Within Dwelling*
- *Chemical Spill*
- *Chipping of Sink*

Source: State Farm

such as a porch or garage. Unattached buildings may be covered as long as they are not used for business or rented to other persons. Building materials on your property may also be covered.

Since the dwelling portion of your policy represents your investment in your home, there are some details of this type of coverage you should understand.

Complete protection against the total destruction of your home obviously requires a policy providing coverage in an amount equal to the replacement cost of the house at current construction prices. Replacement cost is figured as the cost of your home when it was built times a cost trend multiplier, which is an inflation index. By having an inflation endorsement on your homeowners policy, your insurance company will provide automatic increases in coverage, based on slightly increased premiums.

After a total loss by fire, for example, the company would pay only the limits on your policy. This is, however, subject to having your home insured for 80% or more of its replacement cost at the time of the loss.

What this means is that if you carry $20,000 insurance on a $40,000 home and suffer a $10,000 loss, you may get paid only $6,250 if your policy carries the 80% clause. The formula used by many insurance companies is as follows:

Amount insured by you ($20,000)

80% of replacement cost ($32,000) × Amount of loss = ($10,000)

Maximum for which company is liable ($6,250)

Thus, to be reimbursed without penalty in this example, you must be carrying $32,000 (80% of $40,000) at the time of the loss. By starting your policy now at 80% and having the inflation endorsement included, you can avoid the needless worry of keeping pace with inflationary construction costs.

In most cases, a policy you purchased several years ago will no longer reflect the current replacement cost of your home. Unless you take specific steps to raise the value of your homeowners insurance, in keeping with the appreciating value of your property, you could suffer a serious financial loss.

Personal property □ Possessions in your home like clothing and furniture are protected under this section of your policy. Generally these items are covered for their actual value at the time of loss. However, it should be noted that certain items of significant value, like jewelry, may have specified coverage limits. This part of the policy also has some coverage for your personal belongings while you are traveling on vacation, or just away from home.

Medical payments to others □ This pays for medical expenses only for someone who is injured on your property. You may feel morally obligated to pay for someone's injury caused by the property or someone in your household. This coverage does not include payment of medical expenses incurred by you or your family, and carries specified limits.

Supplementary property and liability coverages □ A host of special coverages exist for various situations. If you are aware of them, you can build a policy to include those you feel are particularly valuable for your situation. The two most frequently needed are an automatic inflation endorsement and personal liability coverage above the standard $25,000 limit. Other supplemental coverages protect you against fire department service charges, credit card fraud, liability suit defense costs and first-aid expenses, as well as several other situations. In most cases today these coverages are now automatically included in a homeowners policy.

Peril coverage □ Another factor affecting the amount of premium you pay is the number of threats, or perils, the policy includes. Logically, the greater the number of perils covered, the more expensive the policy. Basic policies cover the most frequently occurring perils; broad policies cover 18 or 19; and comprehensive policies cover all perils except those that are specifically excluded.

Special flood and earthquake coverage □ The U.S. government and the insurance industry together have developed a program to provide insurance to potential flood victims, and coverage has been offered in qualifying communities since 1969. Through the Department of Housing and Urban Development, over 10,000 communities committed to carrying out vital antiflood measures have been approved for the program. Your agent can tell you whether your community is among them. Earthquake insurance is now available throughout the country.

Tailoring your policy □ If you rent rather than own your dwelling, consider renters insurance. You may be pleasantly surprised at how economical coverage can be. Both renters and homeowners can insure personal property of extraordinary value, such as a coin collection, antiques, furs, jewels, art objects, photographic equipment, firearms or the like, if riders are purchased. Riders are specific provisions covering each valuable up to a sum reflecting its real or appraised cost. Also, if you maintain a potential public nuisance on your property, have a high-profile job or own an expensive animal, additional liability insurance is economical protection against a lawsuit.

Insurance discounts □ By following through on the security measures shown in this book, you may qualify your home for special discounts on your homeowners insurance premium ranging from 2% to 10% or more. Check with your agent. As many as three out of four major insurance companies reduce premiums on homes if they have fire and burglary alarm systems.

The biggest discount—from 5% to 10%—is given for homes in which detection devices for burglary and fire report automatically to a UL-listed central alarm monitoring station, where trained operators promptly notify police and fire departments. If the devices are connected directly to police and fire stations, where that is permitted, the usual saving is up to 5% or 6%. If they only sound an alarm on the outside of the house, most companies give up to a 2% discount.

Specific discounts vary according to state, types and numbers of alarms installed, location of house and differing regulations of the various insurance companies. One company may allow a 2% credit for a single UL-listed smoke detector, while another company may allow credit only if one is installed on every living level. In addition to the discounts listed above, some companies provide a 2% to 5% credit for approved sprinkler systems, raising the total for some companies to 15%.

In most instances, the company's representative has to check out the burglary and fire alarm system before the discount is granted. In some cases branch offices are permitted to make larger-than-average discounts for a home protected by an exceptional system.

Watch it, You're Vulnerable!

CHAPTER 2 ■ Of all the threats to the security of your home, the most common is the residential burglar. The odds of your experiencing someone invading the sanctity of your home, seizing part or all of your possessions and vanishing without a trace are increasing dramatically each year.

If your home hasn't been burglarized, chances are that you know of one that has. FBI statistics show that more than one out of every 100 individuals are victims every year. Grim figure? You bet, particularly if you were one of the unwilling contributors to the millions of dollars' worth of loot burglars made off with.

The burglary rate is reaching alarming proportions. In the 18 seconds it's taken you to read this far into this chapter, two more burglaries were added to the total. From 1966 to 1971, for example, burglaries increased 70%. From 1972 to 1976, they jumped another 30%. By 1976, according to the FBI, the annual loss to residential burglars totaled $995 million.

Only 17% of these crimes were solved or cleared up by arrest. In the nation's five largest cities, as many as a third of the burglaries go unreported by citizens who, avoiding the hassle of police paperwork, contribute to high crime rates.

What are the odds of your household being burglarized? In some areas such as Detroit as many as 174 out of 1,000 residences are hit—with burglars operating day and night, showing no marked preference for the hours of darkness over the hours of light. In other cities, rates run even higher, up to 177 per 1,000 in Minneapolis. Only a few major cities, such as Buffalo, Miami, Pittsburgh and Washington, D.C., have burglary rates lower than 100 per 1,000 households. Today most urban Americans can expect to be victims of a burglary or burglary attempt sometime during their lifetime.

One of the worst effects of such crime is the fortress mentality that can develop in communities where victimization rates are high. This mentality leads to self-imposed restrictions, a kind of regimen of fear that can take a great toll in loss of personal freedom and sense of well-being. Even minor crimes can have a major destructive impact on the quality of life in a neighborhood. Vandalism, a crime usually associated with youth and high spirits, actually can affect property values on a long-term basis.

The attitudes developed by successful young vandals may lead to escalating criminal involvement, making burglary one of the fastest-rising crimes in America today. But to really understand what you're up against, you need to get an idea of how a burglar thinks. The following is a behind-the-scenes glimpse at the hows and whys of burglary, through the eyes and ears of Pete Dunham, an inmate at Soledad Prison in California. It's a report on burglary, from burglars' points of view.

"*The money is good, the risk is slight and I'm my own boss.*" The man speaking is Jerry Walcott, a slightly built 30-year-old with wheat-blond hair and penetrating blue eyes. He's a professional burglar, has been for 15 years. Walcott plans to continue his career upon release from prison where he's serving a 2½-year sentence climaxing a crime spree that lasted 12½ years and netted him untold thousands of dollars.

"*I don't believe in robberies because it's necessary to carry a gun and take big chances. In my line of work, the odds against getting hurt or having to hurt someone are minimal.*" Sentenced for second-degree burglary in a large city's Superior Court, he's unrepentant as he serves only a fraction of the six-month to 15-year sentence his crime carries.

Bucky Allen, a high school graduate, full-time burglar and son of an upper-middle-class family says, "*With a large screwdriver and a lot of planning, I can easily net $500 a week or more burglarizing. Tell me where I can earn that kind of money doing anything legal?*" He smiles. "*I couldn't begin to tell you how many stereos, television sets, cameras and typewriters I've stolen in the past five years.*" Bucky is serving only two years and will be released from prison soon. *"Sure. There's a chance I'll be back but I won't do much time and there's no quicker way to make some bread than by ripping off pads."*

Jerry and Bucky are only two of thousands of young and middle-aged men who have found the profits of burglarizing high, the punishment often nonexistent or minimal. For them burglarizing is a way of life, an easy way to make a living. It's an answer to the economic crunch.

While about half of the burglars arrested are juveniles, the other half account for a whole new burglar profile that has radically changed the thinking of criminologists and social scientists. The average burglar in this prison is 27 years old, white and a high school graduate, often with a year or more of college. He comes from a "good" middle- to upper-class family; his parents are still married. He will engage in criminal activities for 20 years, be arrested twice and serve slightly less than five years in prison. He will commit second-degree, or "simple," burglaries (daytime and unarmed) rather than the more serious first-degree, or "aggravated," burglary (often in an inhabited residence with a weapon).

Here's a closer look: *"Many homes and even more professional offices, such as doctor and dentist offices, have what is the easiest lock in the world to crack. The type of lock I can easily beat is the one located in the doorknob. I can get into a place with a lock like that in less than 30 seconds, and nine times out of ten never leave a trace."*

The man talking is Glen Myers, 28, who prides himself on the fact that he's pulled over 3,000 burglaries and has been convicted only once. *"I place a large screwdriver between the baseboard and the frame where the door lock goes into the frame. I give it one good hit with the palm of my hand, then the screwdriver is forced between baseboard and frame. I then pry just a little in that spot, then move it up and down to a foot above and below the lock. I now have the baseboard standing an inch from the frame to which it is nailed. I stick the screwdriver in where the lock enters the frame and apply enough pressure on it to push it back, gently pushing on the door at the same time. After a second or two the lock is far enough back and the door is open. I hit the baseboard three times—once a foot above the lock, once a foot below and finally right even with the lock. It is back exactly the way it used to be except I am now inside a closed and locked home or office."*

Sound like a man who knows what he's doing? He does. Here's

what he says about those popular louvered glass pane windows: "*Another snap are homes that have those slatted windows that are cranked open and shut from the inside. I can be inside within three minutes and nobody's the wiser. For these burglaries I don't even need a tool ... just my fingernail. I've pulled over 200 burglaries in homes that had slatted pane windows and not once did I use a tool. About 99% of the time the windows were completely closed.*"

Glen takes pride in his modus operandi. He boasts about entering homes through openings left by air conditioners that he's removed. "*I simply push the hold arms back, lift the air conditioner out of the window and crawl in.*" Little wonder, with pros like Glen, Bucky and Jerry, that burglaries are on the upswing.

A number of men prefer to work in pairs to carry heavy objects from the house they are burglarizing to their car or truck. John Cado and Jim Reeves, both in their mid-20's, are typical. They burgled for five years before being arrested, and used a system to plan their capers. They had two methods, both very successful.

The first consisted of carefully following the daily crime report in their local newspaper. They would make careful note of the areas in which other burglaries occurred and avoid them because there was apt to be a higher concentration of patrolling police.

Next, they would go to the suburbs, and after knocking on the door of a selected home to make sure no one was there, they would enter the residence. Again referring to the newspaper, they would often select homes whose owners were reported on vacation. More macabre—but thoroughly effective—was burgling homes where deaths had been reported. They would rip off the house on the day of the funeral.

When Cado and Reeves were arrested, the police found their six-room apartment filled from floor to ceiling with stereos, television sets, cameras and other goods with a total worth of $100,000. Their downfall wasn't their methodology, but a curious landlady who lived down the street and often saw them carrying entertainment units and other merchandise into the dwelling.

What separates the full-time professional burglar from his part-time, much less effective brother in crime? "*Instinct and planning are what I count on,*" claims Willie, a man with no last name and every inch a professional. "*If I feel right about a place, I do it no matter what obstacles are in my way. That doesn't mean I would hurt anyone to do the job. I never have and I never would. I just plan jobs more carefully. Of all the places I've ripped off, I've only encountered people in the pad three times, when they returned and surprised me.*

"I never burglarize a home that's occupied. I could get hurt if I ran into the wrong dude, right? And I shy away from places that can only be entered through the front, are on a busy street, are well lit on a semi-busy street or are well lit in a neighborhood with snoopy old ladies living across from them. Them old ladies are a hard lot to put anything over on!

"My fence gives me 50% to 70% of the value on the goods I rip, which is damn good. We've been doing business for a long time. I've gotten as much as $400 for a color television that retails for $500 and as little as $275. My fence is above average though. Most guys get 25% to 50%. I've seen a guy drop a beauty worth six bills for $100 in lean times."

And what does the "average" burglar seek when he enters a home? The list of items most sought remains constant. Stereos, television sets, typewriters (especially electric ones), cameras, movie projectors, jewelry and, of course, cash. (Cash, however, is rarely found in impressive amounts.) Handguns are often taken and fenced to robbers.

Most burglars will not take items they know to be marked. The markings, if discovered, help speed identification and return of stolen goods. Most fences won't handle goods engraved with identification numbers.

Burglars also pass by homes where there is noise or light inside. The barking of a dog is another risk they shy away from. *"Give me a pad with no lights, no noise and no dog and I'll take it off in a minute,"* boasts veteran burglar Mike Holland. *"I don't mess around with anything chancy. You're only inviting disaster if you advertise to burglars you have gone on vacation or that your home is unoccupied for one reason or another!"*

What can you do to avoid contributing to these burglars' standard of living? A fundamental principle behind controlling crime is the removal of the opportunity to commit crime. This principle can often be seen in operation. Many rapid transit systems, for example, have abandoned the practice of making change for bus riders, eliminating the need for drivers to carry cash and thereby taking the payoff out of robbing them. Some launderettes equip their machines to accept only tickets or tokens rather than coins.

A recent government study of several California communities provides some hints. The study showed what the following specific home-security measures accomplish.

Installing alarms □ More than 13 times as many burglaries occurred where there were no alarms in place and functioning (93% vs. 7%).

Marking property □ More than 10 times as many burglaries occurred where the victims were not enrolled in Operation Identification (OPID) or some similar program of marking possessions (91% vs. 9%).

Keeping dogs □ More than 10 times as many burglaries occurred where there were no dogs (91% vs. 9%).

Making entries visible □ Over twice as many burglaries occurred at entry points that were not visible from the street (70% vs. 30%).

Lighting entries □ Over twice as many burglaries occurred at unlighted points of entry (69% vs. 31%).

Lighting streets □ Almost twice as many burglaries occurred where streetlights were 100′ or more from the point of entry (65% vs. 35%).

No one can guarantee that your home won't be burgled even if you take steps to prevent it. But experts—and burglars themselves—agree there are many precautions you can take to lessen the odds.

Strategies to Beat a Thief

CHAPTER 3 ■ If a burglar is really determined to get into your house, it is next to impossible to keep him out. But it is possible, in many small but effective ways, to delay him long enough that he will seek easier prey. Because of the nature of their business, burglars have to hurry. Getting in and out speedily is their best defense. By making access to your home awkward and time-consuming, you greatly reduce the odds of breaking and entering.

A house clearly visible to neighbors is an advantage. You may have to sacrifice a bit of your highly prized privacy, but hedges and overgrown shrubs provide ideal cover for a burglar. A would-be intruder, eyeing houses from the street, will look for a foliage-screened, darkened window as his easiest target. Your neighbor's prying eyes are better than a burglar's.

If your property is separated from the street by a fence, you can attach a set of bells to the gate down low and out of the way. The ringing can be a pleasant way to announce visitors during the day and an alarming development for a burglar at night. Looking at the houses in your neighborhood from a burglar's point of view, would you pick the house with a picket fence out front where you'd have to negotiate a noisy gate with your arms full of loot?

A stand of thorny rosebushes can be just as effective as a brick wall, but don't plant bushes or trees within 5′ of your home's entrance. If your house is not shaded by shrubbery, a light burning outside the front door through the night will help make your home a bad risk.

LIGHT

■ The next time you drive through your neighborhood at night, take a look around from the burglar's point of view. Remember that darkness offers concealment, and from a concealed position a burglar can take his time with the job.

What kind of house will the burglar pass up? One that has light fixtures illuminating the front entrance, the garage and driveway, the back door and the natural approaches to the house. Streetlights help, and some wide-angle floodlights mounted high up on the house and garage walls offer even more protection. If you normally arrive home after dark, you can use timers or photoelectric sensors at the fixtures to turn on the lights at dusk.

If you do not have emergency exterior lighting, then consider mounting a high, effective floodlight on each side of the house. You may not use these often, but many a working burglar has been startled and has fled when lights are suddenly turned on him.

Any light source, even a full moon, acts as a deterrent to burglars. It's a lot easier for a thief to get past your door locks if it's dark and he can take his time without fear of being noticed. Light inside the house also acts as a deterrent to the burglar simply by convincing him that the house is occupied and that he should try elsewhere.

In general, try to avoid rigid schedules. Lights that go on and off at the same time every day can indicate a pattern that a burglar can take advantage of. When you're away, consider having lights turned on and off with timers. Stagger timers in living and bedroom areas.

LOCKS

■ Only a relatively small percentage of burglars bother to pick locks. Windows usually offer less difficult access. All easily reachable windows are good candidates for key locks.

If a window lock is used and the burglar breaks out the glass, he will be unable to move the sash. If your sash does not have crosspieces and the glass is large enough for a man—or child—to crawl through, you have a more serious problem. You can consider a steel or iron grate or a professional jeweler's gate, if legal in your area. Remember, however, that grills and gates can keep you inside in the event of a fire; such devices should open from the inside.

Sash locks on double-hung windows can be jimmied open and are

Low-Cost Thief-Proofing

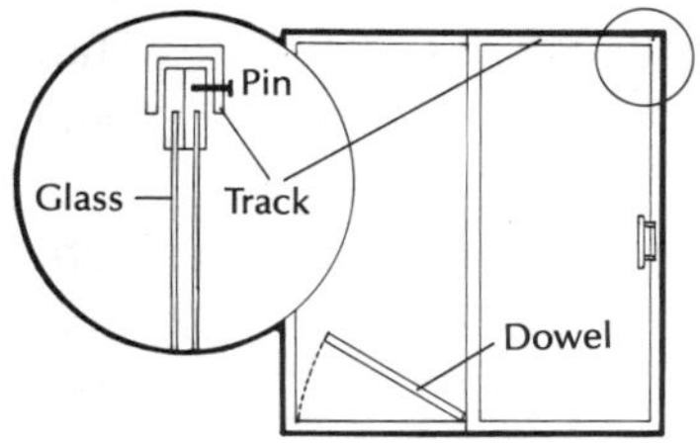

Sliding glass doors can be fortified with 3/4" dowel or short pin. Measure distance between side frame and side edge of sliding panel. Cut dowel 1/4" shorter than measurement, then simply lay it into sliding track between panel and frame.

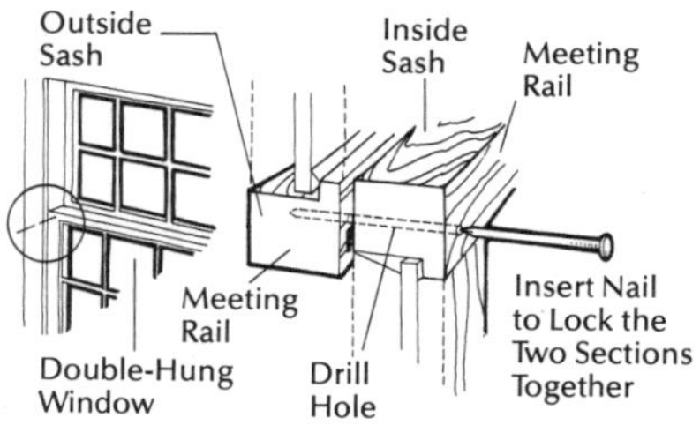

Simple double lock for double-hung windows is possible with common nail. Drill hole through meeting rail of inside sash and partway into outside sash. Inserting the nail locks the two sections together so that neither one can be moved.

a weak link in the security chain. It's simple to back up these locks in a way that's undetectable from outside the house. Drill a hole near the window frame through the meeting rail of the lower sash and halfway through the upper sash while the window is fully closed. Insert a common nail (not a thin finishing nail) into the hole, and the two sash sections are locked together. They can't slide up or down, even if the sash lock is jimmied.

The locks on sliding glass patio doors are smaller and not as sturdy as conventional door locks, and can easily be bypassed by an experienced burglar. Back up the lock with commercially available lock devices. You can also use a dowel or broom handle laid flat in the door track between the sliding panel and the frame, making the door impossible to open whether it's locked or not—a burglar can force the door only an inch or so. The dowel can be conveniently removed when you're in the house.

Keep in mind that if a burglar is screened from view and willing to make noise, he may break out enough glass to crawl through. If you are really concerned about your patio doors, a steel sliding gate is the best answer.

While windows are the most vulnerable means of entry, many doors are easily forced. If your door frames are old or ill fitting, it may be easy to force them with a crowbar. A little repair carpentry can strengthen them. Consider adding metal edging strips to make the use of prying devices and access to locks more difficult.

If your exterior doors are divided into panels that have centers that could easily be broken through, consider bolting a heavy plywood or metal sheet to the inside or outside. With a little decorating imagination, plus paint and molding, you can disguise such a panel. A simpler solution is to use a metal bar inserted in clips on the door jamb across the middle of the panel. Remember that locks are available that must be unlocked from the inside as well as the outside, frustrating the burglar who breaks a hole in the door and reaches in to snap the lock open.

Most of today's standard new doors come equipped with knob locks which offer little protection. A second, deadbolt-type lock should be added to all such doors. Peepholes in your front and back doors are a worthwhile and small expense. They are commonly shaped to give you a broad view of the outside despite their tiny size, and are safer than chain locks which may give way if weight is suddenly thrown against them.

DON'T INVITE TROUBLE

■ Most burglars pick homes at random. Why would a burglar pick yours? It might be the inadequate lighting or the coin collection you display on a table in front of the bay window. But maybe you sent him an invitation.

For example, let's say it's a hot summer day and you're off to the beach. You've turned off the air conditioners and pulled the blinds to keep out the hot sun. It's as though you left a note on the front door: "Nobody's home and we won't be back for quite a while." A house should never look closed down. Leave a window shade partially open or drapes a little separated.

Window air conditioners are risky, especially temporary or seasonal installations. Some can be pried out and stolen, leaving a gaping hole for access to the house. A TV, stereo or camera equipment left in view of a picture window makes your house a prime target for a burglar cruising the area. Keep your valuables out of the public's line of sight.

Although really important items should be kept in a safe or safe-deposit box, there are "safes" built into your house already that you can use. For small items you can use the space in the wall cavity between studs. How? Remove a short section of baseboard molding and cut away a small section of wallboard or plaster to expose the cavity. Install kitchen cabinet friction catches, and the molding sec-

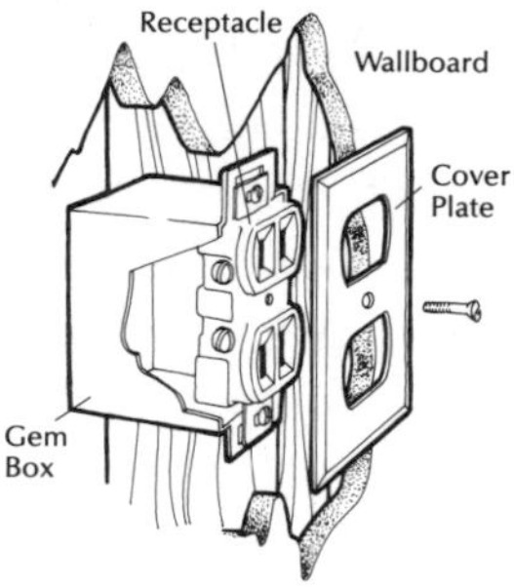

Built-in "safe" can be camouflaged behind fake outlet or wall switch. Cut hole and install a metal electrical box, switch or receptacle as you normally would. Then leave out the wires. Behind the cover plate is a mini-safe.

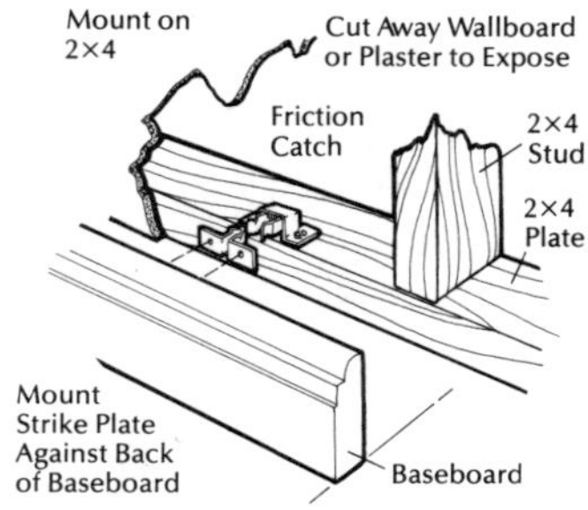

Wall cavity "safe" can help foil burglars who don't have much time. Carefully remove section of baseboard molding, cutting away wallboard to create wall cavity. Replace nails with friction catch to hold panel in place.

tion becomes your secret panel. Not many burglars have the time to go through all your closets, drawers and cupboards and then remove every piece of molding from the wall.

Using the camouflage approach, you can also install a fake light switch or outlet. Cut a hole at the same height as other receptacles, fit in an electrical box and install a toggle switch or outlet. With the cover plate on top everything looks normal, but inside there are no wires—only a convenient little safe. When you start looking around the house you'll find many more built-in spaces behind staircase kickboards, above acoustical-tile suspended ceilings and similar places.

Beware of repeated telephone calls that are wrong numbers. Once a burglar has picked out your house he'll try to establish when you're in and when you're out. A standard procedure for the thief is to call your house from a nearby phone and let it keep ringing as he makes the trip to your door. If he still hears the phone, he's home free.

He might even stop by to get a closer look, asking for directions and at the same time making a quick check of the places many homeowners still regard as safe locations for the extra door key, such as under the mat, in the mailbox, on top of the door trim, in the flowerpot. Burglars know them all.

Some homeowners make it easy. You may have a stamp collection, piece of jewelry or some other item that you want to sell. If your ad in the local paper reads something like "One-of-a-kind stamp collection, serious collectors only, call after 6 P.M.," the burglar (that's right, they read the ads too) can assume he's got a good chance of taking it off your hands sometime before 6:00.

If you frequently get deliveries during the day that are left in conspicuous places until the evening, you're helping the burglar determine your schedule. Try to arrange a delivery to a neighbor's house or at least to a back door that can't be seen from the street.

Noise acts as a deterrent during the day the way light does at night. It's another sign of activity that tells the burglar you may be home. You may not want to leave a radio playing all day, but it's not a bad idea during short absences.

IDENTIFY YOUR PROPERTY

■ Property identification programs encouraged by law-enforcement agencies are based on the principle that if your name and phone number or other identification are engraved onto a stereo or TV set, a burglar will have trouble getting rid of them. If a burglar has a fence for his goods, he may find it difficult to get rid of labeled loot. So he will be less likely to take the property in the first place. However, identifying property is less effective if the criminal's clientele happens to be made up of customers he meets in bars or on street corners.

Many police departments will lend you the tools to do the engraving or at least give you advice on how to proceed (see Chapter 6). Some provide stickers that advertise the fact that your property is marked and easily traceable.

Less than 20% of residential burglaries are solved. If you are robbed, property identification may help the police put a burglar out of commission and improve your chances of getting your property back. As added protection, keep a record of the serial numbers of valuable property in a safe place to use for positive identification.

SIMPLE PRECAUTIONS

■ The days you are on vacation are when your house is most vulnerable since the chance of your leaving a telltale sign to a burglar is greatly increased. The National Sheriff's Association recommends that you follow these simple procedures before leaving:

■ Discontinue newspaper or other deliveries or have them picked up daily by a neighbor.

- Notify the post office to hold your mail until you return.
- Have the grass cut or snow removed, as you would if you were home. A snowdrift across the front steps is a dead giveaway.
- Deposit any extra cash in the bank. If possible, store other valuables in a safe-deposit box just in case.
- Store empty garbage cans in a garage, shed or basement. Out front, they advertise the fact that the house isn't being used.
- Set thermostats to maintain a reasonable temperature, around 80°F in summer and 55°F in winter. No one would be living in a house with frost on all the windows.
- Turn down the bell volume control on your telephone or even smother it with a pillow so the unanswered ringing can't be heard outside the house. This can stymie the burglar's system of calling and letting the phone ring until he gets to your house.
- Leave shades and drapes slightly opened. Don't let the house appear closed up.
- Check all locks on windows and doors, and block the tracks of sliding glass doors to prevent entry even if the lock is successfully jimmied.
- Install a timer that will turn some lights on and off to simulate normal use. The idea is to make your home look as if it is occupied. It doesn't take a very smart burglar to figure out that you have left a single light burning in one room while you are on vacation.
- If possible, leave a key along with a telephone number where you can be reached with a trusted neighbor who can check your house regularly. Let them park a car in your driveway or have their kids play in your yard. An active household discourages burglars.
- Always notify your local police at least one day before you leave and tell them how long you'll be gone. In many communities they will arrange to send a car past your house on a regular basis until you return. Not too many burglars will invest much time casing a neighborhood where they keep spotting a patrol car.

As well as taking precautions when you're away, here's what you can do to protect your home when you're there:

- Never leave out a checkbook or spare wallet containing any important documents such as a duplicate driver's license or credit cards. You are inviting disaster if an uninvited guest spots both the I.D. and blank checks.

■ Mark all of your high-risk property, including stereos, television sets, watches, cameras, tape decks and typewriters by engraving your driver's license or Operation Identification number in an inconspicuous place.

■ If you return to your residence and surprise a burglar, don't try to apprehend him and don't panic. Chances are he's as scared as you and wants nothing more than to get away. Carefully note what he looks like and what he's wearing, and write down this information for the police.

■ If you have a mailbox outside your home, invest in a good lock and keep your mailbox locked at all times. This is especially important if you receive regular monthly payments such as Social Security checks.

■ Check your "doggy doors" and chimneys to see if they are large enough to permit a small burglar to enter. A locked grating on top of your chimney will act as a handy deterrent.

■ If you own handguns, lock them to a solidly fastened display case or keep them locked in a safe or secured drawer.

■ Keep windows and doors locked even when you're inside and never leave the house without locking everything. If you live in a problem area, be vigilant; remain alert to strangers prowling around a neighbor's house. Encourage your neighbors to join you in watching your home.

Many people leave themselves open to burglary. Precautions can make your home a very bad risk for burglars. Even if you observe all the rules for top security, or go a step further and install electronic equipment, never become smug or satisfied. Vigilance, caution and care are the basic requisites for a secure home.

How to Lock Doors

CHAPTER 4 ▪ More than a billion locks of every shape and kind guard America's homes, apartments, stores, offices and factories. And yet our "national security" is alarmingly poor if you look at the forced-entry and burglary statistics—more than 60% of illegal entries occur through apparently locked doors.

Criminal studies show 85% to 90% of all crimes against property are "crimes of opportunity" that happen in less than two minutes. These include breaking into a house, an offense that surged by 36% in the daytime and 23% at night between 1972 and 1976.

According to the National Bureau of Standards, U.S. Department of Commerce, most intruders will try to get through the doors before resorting to the windows. Having the right kinds of doors, locks, frames and hinges increases your chances of keeping burglars out. The safest door has a solid core of wood or is all metal, without a window. A solid-core wood door 1¾" should offer adequate protection against forced entry, says the NBS.

A stronger door with a steel frame that won't splinter can be a deterrent to common, through-the-door burglaries. All-metal security doors usually come with their own steel frames. You simply remove the old frame, install the new one and hang the door. Many exterior replacement doors save energy as well. Such doors can be fitted with add-on deadbolt locks, or you can buy replacement security doors which have self-locking hinges, latch and up to three deadbolts.

How Burglars Enter Your Home

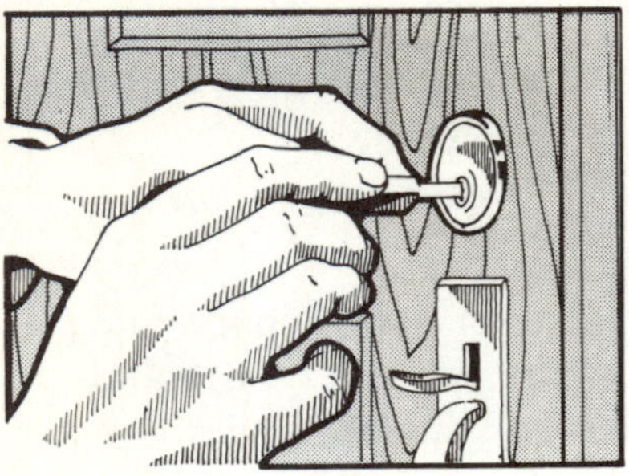

Picking. Skilled burglar opens lock with picking tools; no evidence of forced entry. Quick, quiet—greatest threat to your safety.

Frame spreading. All it takes is thief with portable jack to spread door frame, leaving bolt loose and home unprotected.

Jimmying. Thief forces lock with large screwdriver or crowbar and brute strength. Most common way of gaining unlawful entry.

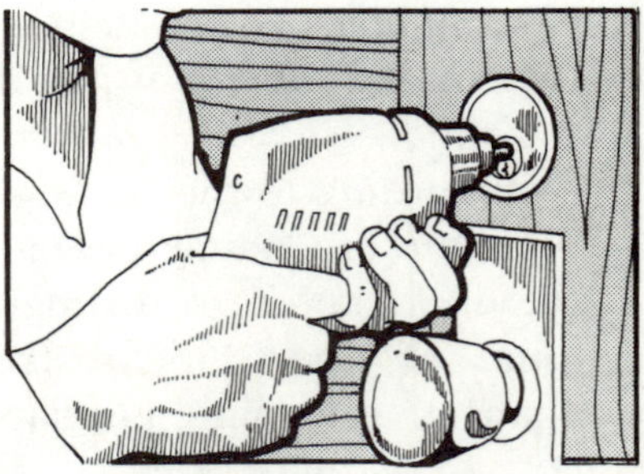

Drilling. Even an amateur burglar can drill through locking pins with portable power tool, destroying your security.

Wrenching. Any novice using pipe wrench can twist cylinder out of door lock and be in your home in five minutes or less.

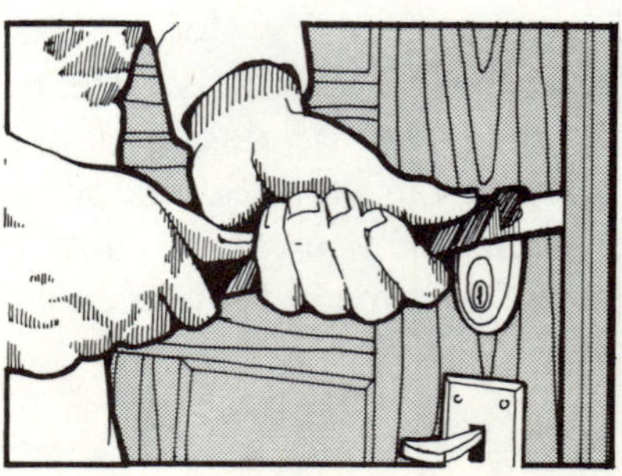

Hacksawing. Thief slips hacksaw blade between door and frame, cuts right through bolt to gain easy entry into your home.

SECURING DOORS

■ There are inexpensive ways to beef up hollow-core doors. You can cover the interior side with 1/2″ plywood, which is then painted, stained or decorated. For more protection, first cover the inside with a sheet of galvanized metal, then cover that with plywood. Reinforce the hinge plates too. Take out the old screws and replace them with countersunk wood screws at least 3″ long.

One of the most common ways a burglar breaks through doors is by breaking the strike out of the door frame. The strike is the metal plate attached to the side of the door frame where the bolt latches

This steel security door with conventional but stylish design discourages break-ins. Steel frame around door opening helps prevent forced entry, while special weatherstripping and foam core provide tight weather seal.

the door. The screws used to attach the strike to the frame are often too short, making it easy to break loose the strike from the frame. Screws long enough to go through the frame and into the wall studs make the strike more burglar-resistant. Also a longer-than-normal strike secured by long screws is harder to break out of the frame.

Burglars often break through the glass in and around doors to reach in and open the door from the inside. If your home has glass large enough to reach through and within 40″ of the doorknob or any locking part of the door, take extra precautions. The glass should either be covered with protective grillwork or replaced with laminated glass, acrylic plastic or polycarbonate plastic. For more protection you can cover the window openings with 3/4″ plywood, which you can paint or decorate. Windows that are close to doors should also be screened or covered.

A well-mounted heavy security chain can help delay forced entry through an exterior door. But all solid doors should have a 180° peep sight or other viewing device in them. Inferior versions let a criminal crouch down and remain unobserved. Peep sights are not expensive and are easily installed. Chapter 14 shows how to use closed-circuit TV.

Jalousie doors (doors with glass slats that angle out) also pose problems. It is possible for a burglar to manipulate the crank or knob that opens the glass section from outside the door. You can prevent this by removing the knob or lever when it is not in use. You can also drill a small hole through both the housing and the shaft of the knob or lever. Then you can insert a pin through the hole to prevent the crank from being turned.

Sliding glass patio doors can often be removed by lifting them from the grooves they slide in, even from the outside. Spacers or protruding screw heads can be installed in the grooves over the door to prevent this type of removal. Many patio doors have rather weak latches which can easily be broken by prying the door away from the frame. A piece of pipe or broom handle in the bottom grooves can prevent the door from being opened if the latch is broken. You may also want to add a stronger-than-normal lock to these doors. Chapter 5 shows devices you can buy to fortify patio doors.

The way conventional wooden door frames (or jambs) are attached to the wall can also pose a security problem. Often a space between the door frame and the wall studs (the part of the wall to which the frame is attached) allows the frame to be spread, thus disengaging the lock. You can put wood spacers between the frame and studs where the hinges are attached. If you have a metal doorframe installed in a masonry wall, be sure the space between the jamb and wall is filled with mortar.

After you reinforce doors, check door hinges. A well-secured hinge protects a home against two types of entry: 1) forcing the door out of the frame by applying pressure to the hinged side, and 2) removing the hinge pins and lifting the door out of its frame.

A door that opens outward is less vulnerable than one that opens inward because it is much more difficult to pull a door out of its frame than to push it in. However, if the door does open outward, the hinge pins are accessible. If they are removed, the door can easily be taken out of its frame. You can replace them with hinges that have fixed pins, or secure the door as follows: Put a screw or nail into the back edge of the door at a point halfway between the sets of hinges, allowing it to protrude about 1/2″. Drill holes in the door jamb to accept the protruding nail or screw. Even if the hinge pins are taken out, the door cannot be removed.

CHOOSING LOCKS □ Locks can be divided into two basic kinds: surface locks and those that are installed within or through the door. Surface locks include safety chains, sliding bolts, bars of various sorts—any lock that is fixed to the door surface.

The main failing of a surface lock is that it can be ripped off the door if enough force is applied. It relies only on the holding power of several screws, and a strongly directed shove may be enough to tear the screws right out of the door. To prevent this, fasten surface locks in place with long, heavy screws that are coated with glue before being driven into the wood. A door should have a well-mounted, heavy security chain and/or through bolts. And the door and frame should be solid and close fitting.

Key-in-knob locks □ The most common through-the-door locks used by builders today, these are locks with the keyhole in the knob. They have a spring-actuated latch that is beveled on one side to allow the door to close. Locksmiths don't like key-in-knob locks because the knob can be forced and broken, exposing the locking mechanism. If you now have a key-in-knob lock, you would be wise to install a second deadbolt lock above it on the door, or a deadlocking latch which prevents the latch on the lock from being forced back when the door is closed.

In general, key-in-knob locks offer little challenge to anyone seriously interested in breaking in. An amateur burglar can simply hack

Types of Door Locks

Since the cylindrical lock has been perfected, mortise locks have had a drop in popularity. They are somewhat costly to install—mortising out relatively large sections of door may be necessary.

Rim locks, usually installed above existing locks, are less expensive than through-the-door types. Generally a good in-the-door entry lock with a deadbolt is considered superior for added security.

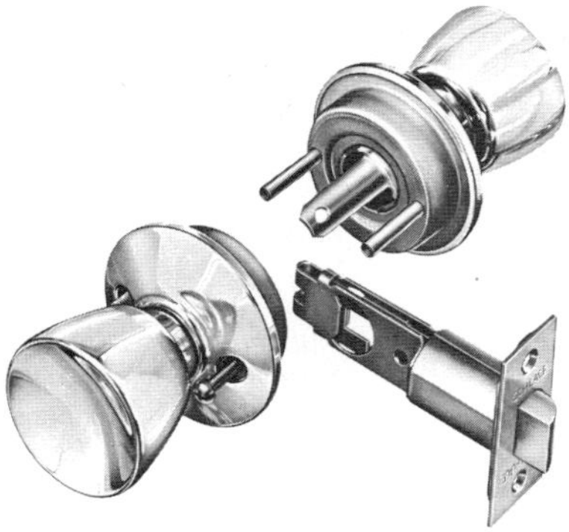

Tubular lock has minimum number of working parts. It often lacks the strength and smooth action of more sophisticated cylindrical locks, but is acceptable for interior doors and for exterior doors when security from forced entry is a consideration.

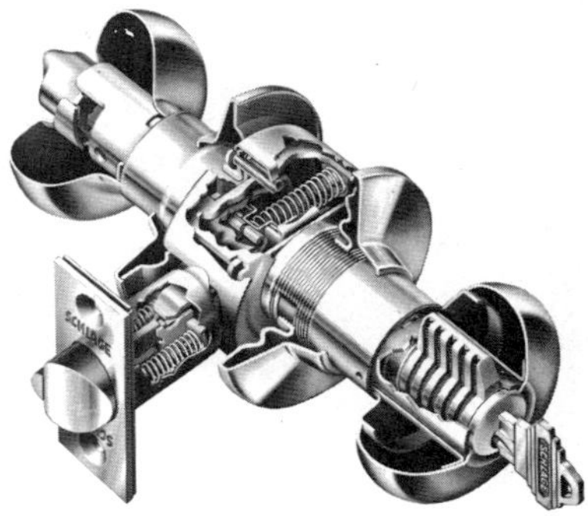

This cylindrical lock is considered a quality heavy-duty residential lock. For safety, entrance locks like this one have "panic-proof" feature allowing for exit with turn of inside knob. An auxiliary deadbolt lock boosts security from forced entry.

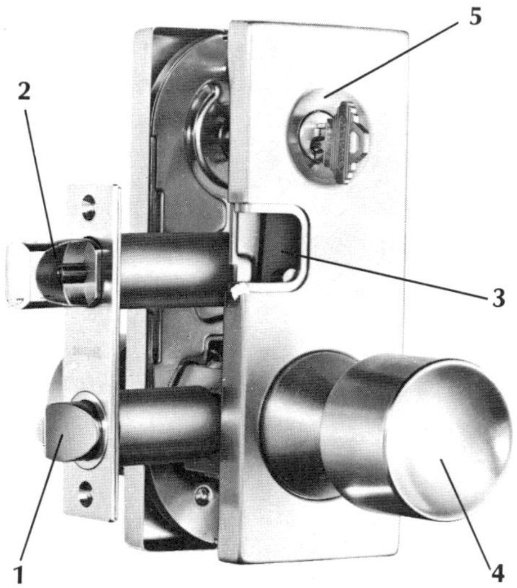

Combination spring bolt and deadbolt lock set provides double-locking protection. Parts include: 1 and 2) latches with ½"- and 1"-throw deadbolts; 3) armor plate to protect mechanism; 4) outside knob that free-spins when locked; and 5) recessed cylinder. Permits turn-of-knob exit for safety.

away at the doorknob with a heavy object or pry the knob loose with a sturdy tool. Since the keying mechanism is within the knob, entry becomes a simple matter once the doorknob is substantially damaged or removed.

Another weak spot is the latch. The shorter the latch the easier it is to jimmy the door open. On most key-in-knob models, the latch extends less than ½". If a door is poorly fitted, there's often too much space between the door edge and jamb. If your door has a

Single-cylinder auxiliary bored deadbolt lock is recommended in addition to other keyed lock sets. It locks automatically when fully thrown and can't be forced by inserting card between door and jamb.

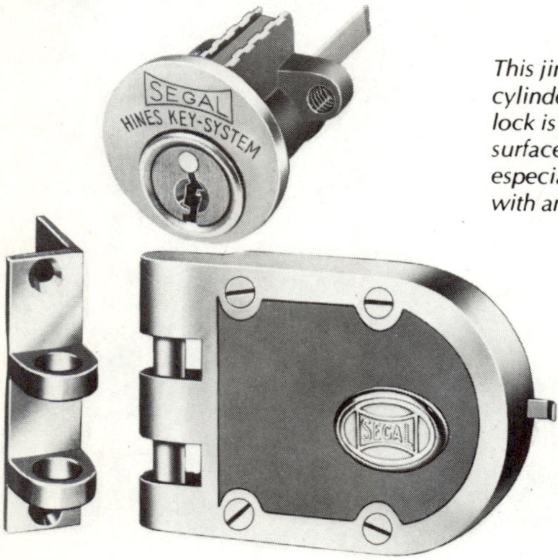

This jimmy-resistant type of cylinder rim vertical deadbolt lock is the most effective of surface-mounted locks, especially since it is equipped with antipick cylinder.

typical 1/16″ of space between the edge and jamb and is equipped with a lock that has a latch extending slightly less than 3/8″, the latch goes only a little more than 1/4″ into the jamb. That's not much protection against jimmying.

If you're buying a new house that's not yet built, or if you're replacing an entrance door, shun the key-in-knob lock. The cheapest and easiest way to increase your security is to add an auxiliary lock.

If you feel you have no reason to fear professional burglars but are concerned about kids or inexperienced intruders, you might prefer, for appearance and convenience, a heavy-duty substitute for a standard key-in-knob lock already on your door. Otherwise, it just doesn't make much sense to buy a heavy-duty model as a replacement. The good ones are different enough in size that a locksmith would have to rework the door cavity. Once you've decided on that expense, you might as well put in a mortise lock and substantially upgrade your security.

Mortise locks □ These locks are set in a rectangular cavity cut into the door edge. They have both a spring latch and a deadbolt; the spring latch can be locked by buttons in the door edge. Most mortise locks are operated by a key from the outside and turning knob on the inside, although you can buy models with keys on both the inside and outside for use in doors with windows. With a lock of this type, remember that you are locked in and must have a key to get out. In case of a fire or other emergency, this could be a problem. You must have a key hanging inside, near the door, but out of the sight and reach of a burglar.

Beveled bolts can easily be opened with a credit card or very thin piece of plastic. The bolts on mortise locks are not beveled, so they can't be carded. Furthermore, the bolts are quite hefty and extend $1/2''$ or more into the door jamb, offering good resistance to jimmying. But if there's excessive clearance between the door edge and

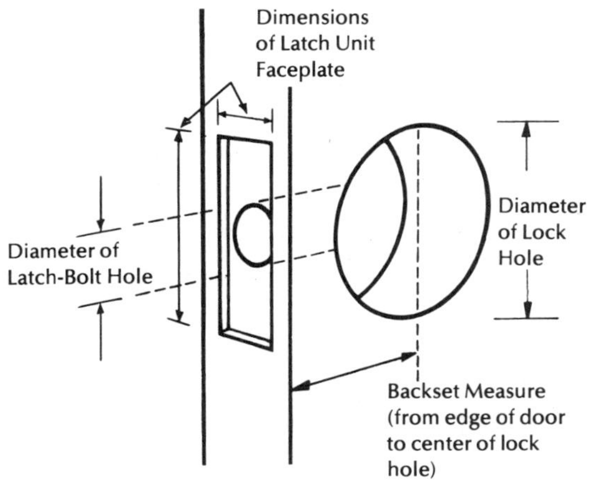

You should be able to install either tubular or cylindrical-bored locks yourself. When replacing, write down type of original lock, its manufacturer, door thickness and dimensions as shown here.

jamb, a mortise lock becomes easy to jimmy. To deal with the problem of poor door fit, some locks have face plates that can be angled to minimize the clearance between door and jamb.

Mortise locks do have some drawbacks. One comes from misuse rather than from design. The beveled convenience latch on most mortise locks is not intended to keep the door securely locked; that's the bolt's job. But you can set the latch so that it locks when you close the door. Since it then takes a key to open the latch from outside, you may mistakenly believe that your home is secure when you close the door. It isn't. A mortise lock with a latch not guarded by a trigger bolt can be carded, or shimmed. To be secure, mortise types must be locked with the bolt, not with the latch alone. A typical mortise is bolt locked from the outside only when you turn the key, never when the door is simply closed. The bolt is locked from the inside only when you throw the thumb turn.

Some mortise locks have one other potential weakness. If the lock cylinder is held in position by a setscrew in the lock face on the edge of the door, someone could loosen it in a matter of seconds—in the time, say, it would take you to answer the telephone while a stranger is left waiting at the open door. Once the setscrew is loose—something you're unlikely to notice—the cylinder can be removed from outside the door. Then a burglar can release the bolt and latch with his finger or a small tool. Some locks have protective plates that cover the setscrews. If not, put a dab of putty or epoxy on the screw heads.

The best-quality mortise locks have bolts and latches that extend more than 1/2″ and are really solid. Shorter locks with less heft should be passed up if it's real security you're after.

Rim locks □ These are surface mounted on the inside of the door. A cylinder extends through the door to the outside where the lock is opened by a key. According to locksmiths, the most secure lock is a vertical bolt mounted on a solid door and equipped with an antipick cylinder.

Adding an auxiliary rim lock is the simplest way to bolster the security offered by your present primary door lock. A vertical-bolt lock is secured to its mating plate in the same way a door hinge is secured by its pin. As a result, vertical-bolt locks are virtually jimmy-proof. When properly installed, they cannot be disengaged from the mating plate unless the lock itself is physically destroyed—and that is a noisy, tough task.

Replacing Key-in-Knob Lock

First remove existing lock from door.

Next remove old latch.

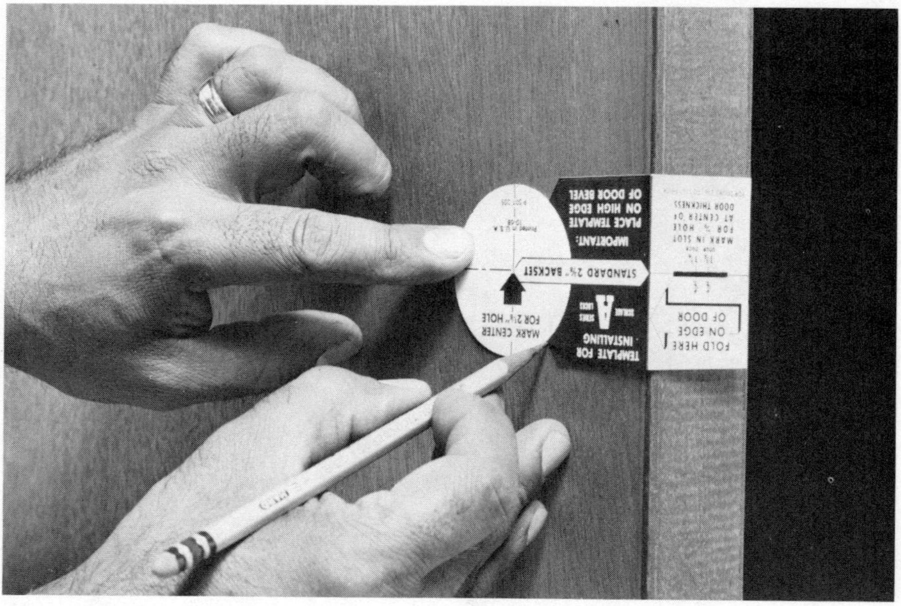

Now use template packed with new lock to mark area to be enlarged.

For a jig like this, use a hole saw to enlarge area for new lock. If new hole requires only minor enlargement, use a wood rasp.

If necessary, cut away excess wood in door edge to accommodate new latch plate.

Next, install new latch in door.

Now insert new lock mechanism from outside door.

Completed installation.

A jimmying burglar might try to dislodge the lock or mating plate from its moorings. But long, coarse-threaded screws secure the lock to the door, and up to seven screws secure the mating plates to the jamb. Unless Superman turns burglar, there's little chance that a thief can tear out the screws from a substantial door or jamb—it would be much easier to tear down the door.

These auxiliary locks use a lock cylinder mounted with a rim nearly flush with the outside surface of the door and an inside thumb turn or lock cylinder. The double-cylinder arrangement provides added security for doors with glass panes or thin wood panels, which can be easily smashed. If there's an inside cylinder instead of a thumb turn, a burglar won't be able to reach through a broken pane and work the lock by hand.

But an inside lock cylinder may be too secure in a fire or other emergency. Remember, you can't get out without a key. If you use such a lock, keep a key in plain sight near the lock but out of arm's reach of the door, and make sure everyone in your family knows where it is and how to use it. Include this precaution in your home fire drills too.

Deadbolt locks □ These are bolts with squared ends, as opposed to spring latches with beveled bolts. With most deadbolt locks, a cylinder is set into the face of the door and only a key will throw the 3/4″ bolt open or closed. Inside may be a turn knob or, if the door has glass windows, a second cylinder. These are known respectively as single- or double-cylinder deadbolt locks.

By using good 1″-throw deadbolt locks that have cylinders protected by special security rings, you will have eliminated break-ins by most amateur and professional burglars. Unless the burglar is sure you are away from home, or your home is in a remote rural area and you've given the burglar a lot of time to work, you will have inconvenienced him enough that he will be far more likely to look for an easier target.

If you ask a locksmith which type of lock is the safest, he'll probably tell you that a good mortised lock set is best. For top security, he might recommend the addition of a vertical-bolt or deadbolt secondary lock to the door as well. You'll need two keys to open the door, which is a nuisance, but you'll have a jimmy-proof, secure door.

The quality of locks varies. Examine locks on display; the machining will tell you a lot. Good locks are smooth and well machined, and work easily. The bolt slides shut with a solid sound and offers such features as case-hardened steel and one-piece construction. Cheap locks look, feel and sound cheap and flimsy.

Whether choosing a primary or secondary type, look for a lock that has a 1″ throw of the bolt. This length bolt will project farther into the strike plate and be much harder to jimmy than a shorter bolt. Locks that throw as little as 1/2″ are easily opened by burglars using a portable jack to spread the door frame.

When buying a lock for an exterior door, don't be economy minded. Spend what it takes to get the best; it's cheap insurance that you can't duplicate after a break-in. The highest-priced locks have both fine finishes and good locking designs.

Cylinders □ Regardless of the type of lock you buy, the cylinder is critical in providing protection. It must withstand efforts by criminals ranging from lock-pick experts to strong-arm burglars.

The cylinder is the part of the lock into which the key is inserted. The most common type of cylinder is the pin tumbler and it works like this: As the key is inserted, spring-loaded pins are raised to the proper position to allow the barrel and the key to turn; the turning causes the bolt or latch (or both) to move. If the wrong key is used, the pins will line up incorrectly and prevent the barrel from turning, thus keeping the latch or bolt solidly in place.

From a security standpoint, a cylinder should have at least six pins. This often results in the cylinder being longer than the thickness of the door. In mortise locks, a six-pin cylinder often extends slightly beyond the surface of the door, thus making it susceptible to forcible removal by use of a gripping tool. To prevent use of such a tool, protruding cylinders should be protected by one of the following:

Spinner ring—a hardened steel ring that forms a collar around the cylinder and spins freely around the cylinder when gripped.

Beveled-ring cylinder guard—a case-hardened steel ring that prevents the cylinder from being gripped by a tool because of its beveled shape.

Escutcheon plate—a metal plate mounted to the door, which covers all of the cylinder except the core (the part where the key is inserted), protecting the cylinder from attack. The escutcheon plate should be attached to the door with one-way screws.

Replacement cylinders for wood doors are available which can be reprogrammed for new tumbler combinations. They eliminate the need for special tools or a locksmith.

Recently, high-security lock cylinders have become available which utilize special keyways and keys to make the cylinder pick-proof. Such cylinders provide improved security from duplication, but may require registered keys that can be duplicated only at the factory upon receipt of a signed request. A compromise is the use of a key type with a blank not available normally, but for which spare blanks are kept as replacements.

Other locks □ An outdoor shed, gate or other portal you want to secure can be protected by a padlock and a tough hasp. There are five basic types of padlock mechanisms. Pin-tumbler and lever-tumbler locks with a hardened steel shackle provide the best protection against picking, hacksawing and jimmying. Disk-tumbler padlocks combine good security and low cost. If stoutly constructed, combination locks spare you the inconvenience of carrying another key and offer excellent security. Warded locks are cheapest, and give only so-so protection. They're best suited to keeping inquisitive youngsters out of places they shouldn't be.

When buying a padlock, look for a hardened shackle (the word "hardened" will be embossed right into the shackle metal). A quality pin-tumbler lock will have the words "pin" or "tumbler" on the package. Don't match up a quality lock with a shoddy hasp.

Besides padlocks, other devices are available which help back up standard locks and bolts. One device you can buy is wedge shaped, and installs inside the door in a special floor plate.

Padlocks can be helpful in boosting home security. This security plate slips over an ordinary slide bolt and transforms it into a double-lock security system. No tools are needed.

Remember that the best lock is poor protection if you fail to use it correctly. Don't rely on the latch, even when you're going out "just for a few minutes." A watchful burglar can spot you dashing out of the house, with the door slamming shut on its own behind you. He knows that if you didn't take the extra few seconds to insert the key and throw the bolt from the outside, just the latch is securing the door. Every hurdle you put in his way makes your house a poorer prospect for a break-in.

Don't be careless with keys. Don't identify your keys with a name, address or car license-plate number. Know to whom you've given a key and, if one is lost, play safe and have the lock cylinder replaced or repinned by a competent locksmith.

Instead of changing lock cylinders when your keys are lost or stolen, you now can buy replacement door locks which can be reprogrammed to accept up to 1,000 different key changes.

One such lock system handled by Sears, called the Match Key System, includes rim-lock cylinders which replace existing cylinders on front and back doors, a program key and two house keys. If you want to change keys, you buy a new program key and matching house keys. You insert the original program key and turn it 70° to the right. Then you set a new tumbler combination by inserting the new program key, turning it left to the original upright position and removing it. The lock will then accept only the keys that match the new program key. The new program key is kept to clear the tumbler combination if needed. This system costs under $20 for two doors.

What to Do About Windows

CHAPTER 5 ■ Windows usually offer the easiest access to a house, even though most thieves will try the door first. If you live in a suburban or rural area, concentrate on the security of basement windows and windows that can be easily reached from the ground, a porch or a trellis. In urban areas, rear or alley windows, or windows that can be reached from a roof or fire escape should get special attention.

Some low-cost ways of increasing the security of windows are shown in Chapter 3. For example, you can drill holes in double-hung windows and pin the sash sections with a common nail. You can use inexpensive doweling or a broom handle section in the track of sliding glass patio doors to make them impossible to open. Other inexpensive ways of beefing up the security of windows are shown in this chapter. Chapter 12 shows how you can use electronic equipment to fortify windows as well as doors and other potential entry points.

Some newer replacement windows that are on the market incorporate a supplementary security latch in addition to the regular locking latch. The security latch on one unit engages or releases with fingertip pressure to provide double security when the window is closed and locked, while permitting the window to be opened a safe few inches for ventilation.

A variety of inexpensive locks are available for installation on windows. The installation of most of these locks is simple, and often you can install all the locks required in an ordinary home in a single afternoon, with time to spare.

TYPES OF WINDOW PROTECTION

DOUBLE-HUNG WINDOWS □ Sash locks on double-hung windows can be jimmied open. Key locks will help keep intruders from moving the sash even if the glass is broken out.

If the sash of your window does not have crosspieces and the glass is large enough for a man to crawl through, you have a great challenge. You may want to consider a steel or iron grate, or a professional jeweler's gate over windows if they are legal where you live. Remember, however, that as with all lock installations, you want to make sure you have adequate exits in case of fire or other home disasters.

Types of Window Locks

This heavy-duty cam-action catch lock holds windows securely, and can be locked and unlocked only with key. Even if prowler breaks or cuts glass, sash can't be opened.

This lock is for double-hung wood windows, and locks without key. Mounts to sash and is furnished with two lock plates for locking in both closed and ventilating positions. Requires key to unlock.

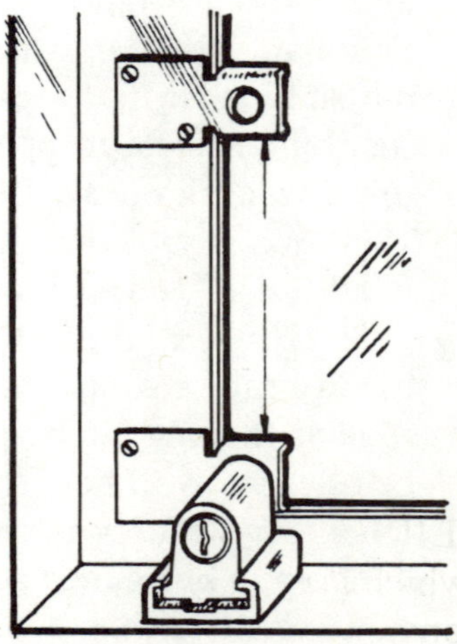

This sash lock may be key-locked open or closed on wood double-hung windows.

This lock for aluminum windows installs easily to give deadbolt protection. Window can be opened only with key, so vandals can't open through broken glass. Window can be locked in open ventilating position.

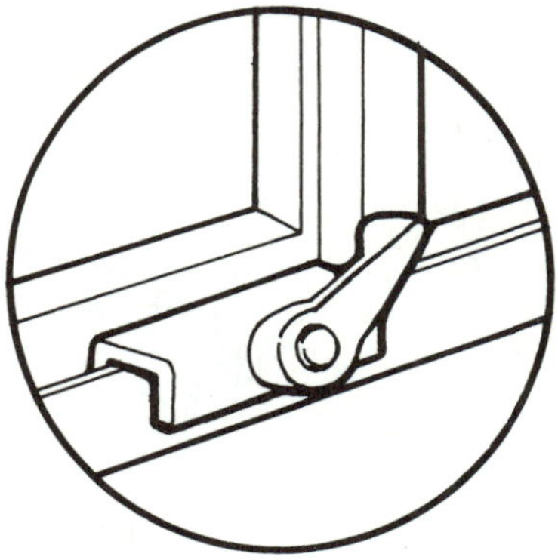

This keyless lock for aluminum windows installs without drilling or tools, and provides viselike grip to help prevent prying; won't, however, protect against "broken glass" entry.

Casement-window key lock easily replaces existing nonlocking casement-window handles. Indicator button shows if it's locked or unlocked. Available for right- or left-handed applications.

SLIDING WINDOWS □ The locks on sliding glass patio doors (which are really just big windows) are smaller and not as sturdy as conventional door locks. They can easily be bypassed by the experienced burglar. Key locks, security pins and special automatic sliding-door closers and locks are available to fortify sliding windows. You can also back up the original lock with a commercially available "Charley-Bar," a device that braces the unit in a locked position.

To go a step further, you can install a sliding gate on the outside. This will help prevent a burglar who is screened from view and

Types of Sliding Glass Window and Door Locks

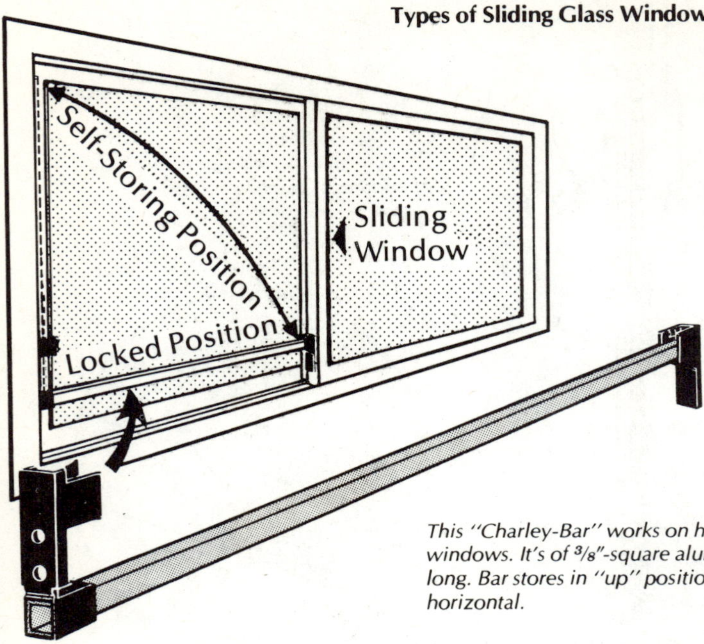

This "Charley-Bar" works on horizontal sliding windows. It's of 3/8"-square aluminum tubing, 36" long. Bar stores in "up" position, locks in horizontal.

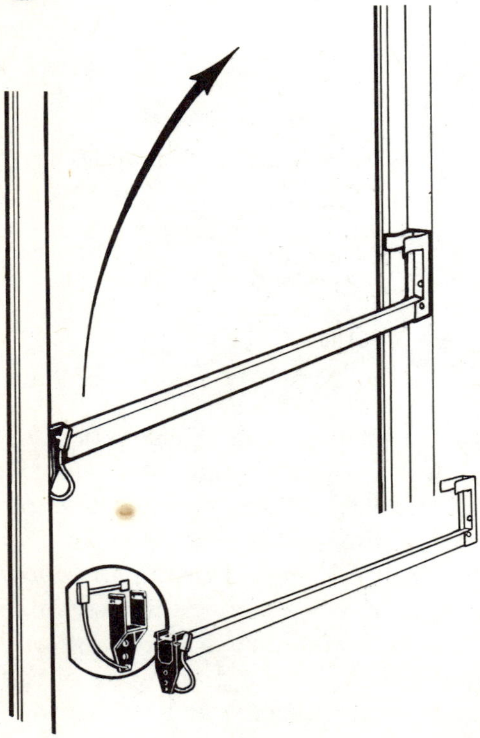

"Charley-Bar" safety lock shown here is quick and easy to install on doors 36" to 48" wide. Attached key locks bar to prevent its being raised from outside by wires. Unit will not protect against entry through broken glass.

This unit automatically closes sliding door and has positive door lock. Installs on inside or outside track, or even on double sliding doors to automatically close after every exit. May be set for partially or fully opened position.

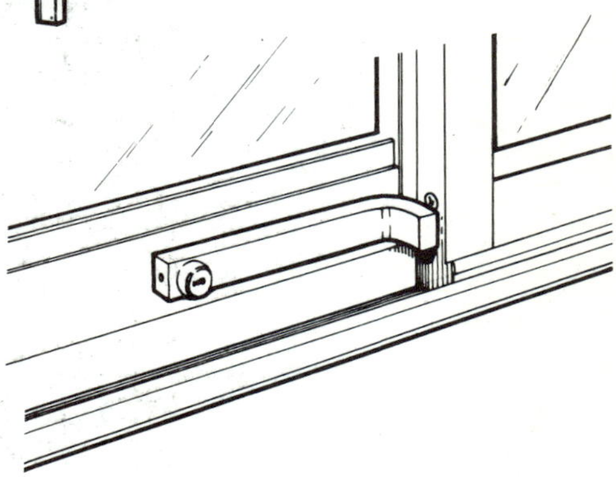

Key lock for sliding doors interlocks both stationary and sliding panel with "sheer action" principle to prevent forced entry by jimmying, complete removal of panels or hand entry through broken glass. Can be installed by drilling three holes.

This patio door lock prevents entry through broken glass. Has steel locking bolt and three mounting screws to provide resistance to prying and lifting. Hand or foot lever operates steel locking bolt.

willing to make a little noise from breaking out enough glass to crawl through.

JALOUSIE WINDOWS □ Experienced burglars will tell you that jalousie windows provide the easiest way to get inside your home. Even a penknife can be used to bend the clip end of the window frame and remove the glass. If you are serious about making your home more secure, consider replacing jalousie windows with a sturdier type. It is also possible to manipulate from the outside the crank that opens glass slat louvers. You can prevent this by removing the crank handle when it is not in use. Or you can drill a small hole through both the housing and the shaft of the crank, and insert a pin through the hole to prevent the handle from being turned.

WINDOW AIR CONDITIONERS □ A common mistake many homeowners make is to install window air conditioners without regard to security. Often this becomes the weakest link in a home-security system. If you use a window-installed air conditioner, take special pains to make sure it can not be easily removed to facilitate entry.

You may want to link the air conditioner to an electronic alarm system. Or investigate ways to use scrap iron, screws, padlocks and other materials to make sure your air conditioner does not invite unwanted intruders. Your local police department or sheriff's office may have specific suggestions for what you can use.

BASEMENT WINDOWS □ Basement windows also require attention since they are by far the most accessible and the least visible windows in most homes. Besides locks, there are several options for boosting basement window security. You can install a protective translucent material such as acrylic over the glass to make it more secure.

You can also use strap iron on the window to make it difficult for a burglar to worm his way through the opening even if the window has been smashed or removed. Use a couple of sturdy metal straps, 1″ wide by 1/4″ thick, that are long enough to reach the frame on both sides. Drill countersunk holes in each end and use long, heavy screws to attach the straps. A burglar will have to risk making noise and go to considerable trouble to get past this arrangement.

If you are not concerned about ventilation, you can replace your basement windows with glass blocks, as shown on page 64. Or, if you don't need either ventilation or light, you can board up or wall over the entire basement window.

GLASS SUBSTITUTES

■ Much of a home's window vulnerability results from the fact that ordinary glass is so easy to penetrate. Besides the less attractive alternatives of walling over or using security grates, you have the option of replacing glass in windows and doors with transparent—but tougher—materials.

Tempered glass is a good glass alternative, but it's expensive and the ordinary homeowner does not have the know-how or tools to cut and handle it. Acrylic plastic is a more feasible substitute. Besides being a heat-saver, acrylic material has a high impact resistance and is safer. It has from 6 to 17 times greater impact resistance than glass and comes in thicknesses of 1/80″ to 1/4″. The thicker the sheet, the greater its impact resistance.

INSTALLING ACRYLIC □ Another advantage of using an acrylic material such as plexiglass is that it is easy to work with. A power saw or inexpensive cutting tool designed for cutting acrylics is all you need. Here's the basic procedure.

To calculate the dimensions of the sheet for the existing opening, you will have to allow for the thermal expansion of the material. Measure the opening. Then subtract the thermal expansion factor from the length and width measurements. If your long measurement is 12″ to 36″, subtract 1/16″. If the long dimension is 37″ to 48″, subtract 1/8″; if it's 49″ to 60″, subtract 3/16″.

Plexiglass can be cut with a circular saw, saber saw or by scribing and breaking. If you are using a circular saw, select a steel crosscut blade of the type recommended for finish cuts of plywood, veneers or laminates. The blade should have six teeth per inch of the same shape, height and point-to-point distance. Set the blade just higher than the thickness of the acrylic to prevent chipping. Do not force-feed. If you are using a saber saw, use a blade with 24 to 32 teeth per inch for material 1/10″ and 1/8″ thick, and 14 to 24 teeth per inch for 3/16″ and 1/4″ material. Scribing and breaking tools for plexiglass and other plastics are available in most hardware stores. Instructions for their use are usually included.

Nonhardening glazing compounds (putty) or silicone sealants should be used when glazing plexiglass because of the material's tendency to expand and contract a little with temperature and humidity changes. State statutes and building codes require the use of safety glazing in hazardous locations such as storm doors. After plexiglass is installed, it should be cleaned with a 1% solution of a mild soap or detergent and water. You can remove tar, grease or paint with a good grade of naphtha or kerosene.

To replace glass in wood sash windows, follow these steps:

1. Remove the wood strips or glazing compound and glass.
2. Measure the opening and subtract the thermal expansion factor.
3. Remember to locate and include the safety glazing label when cutting your sheet to size.
4. Remove the masking paper.
5. Carefully put a thin bead of nonhardening elastic putty or silicone sealant around the inside of the rabbet, and press the plexiglass pane in place.
6. If you are using wood strips to hold your pane, replace them.
7. If you are using a glazing compound, fasten the pane in place with glazier's points 5″ or 6″ apart.
8. Lay a smooth triangular line of glazing compound in the rabbet with a glazing trowel or a putty knife.

To replace glass in a door, proceed as follows:

1. Remove the frame with the glass from the door.
2. Measure the door opening and subtract your thermal expansion factor.
3. Locate the permanent safety glazing label on the edge of the sheet. Material that is 3/16″ or 1/4″ thick is usually required.
4. Trim the sheet to size; make sure you don't cut off the labeling.
5. Sand the edges with medium-grit (60–80) paper to remove any saw marks.
6. Remove the protective masking and install the unframed plexiglass right in the opening.
7. Tighten the clips until snug, just as you would for a frame.

Replacing Glass with Plexiglass Pane

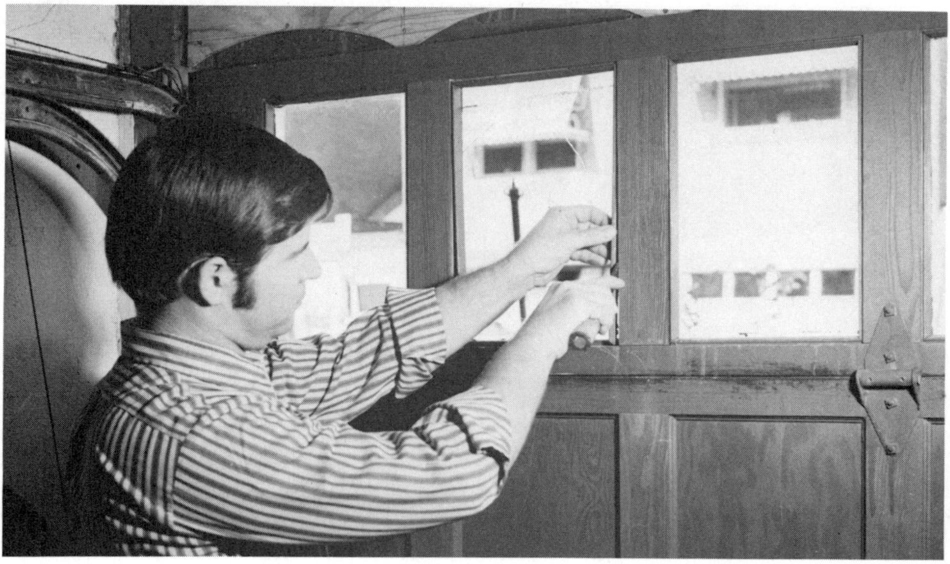

Here's how plexiglass is installed to put an end to broken garage-door windows. The first step is to remove wood strips or glazing compound (putty) and broken glass.

When scribing and breaking plexiglass, use a good cutting tool. Scribe plexiglass several times —five or six passes of blade for 1/10" and 1/8" thicknesses; seven to ten times for 3/16" and 1/4" thicknesses.

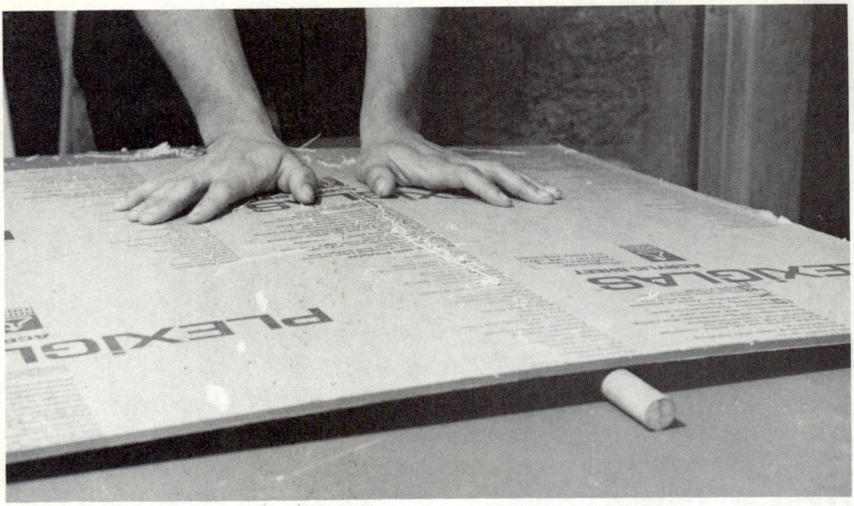

After scribing, place scribed line face up over 3/4" wood dowel. To break, hold with one hand and apply pressure downward on short side of cut with the other.

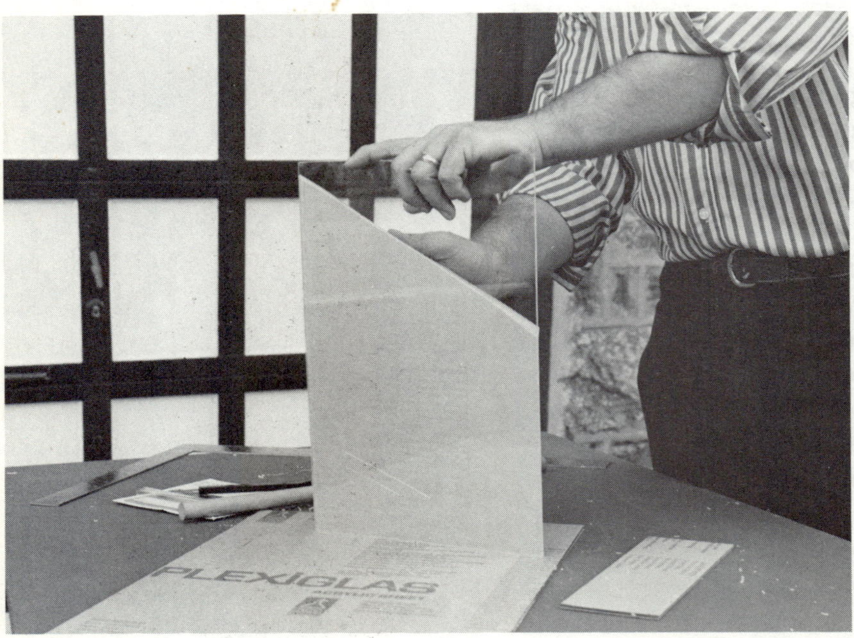

Measure opening and subtract thermal expansion factor. Trim sheet to size and sand edges to round slightly with medium-grit sandpaper. Remove protective masking.

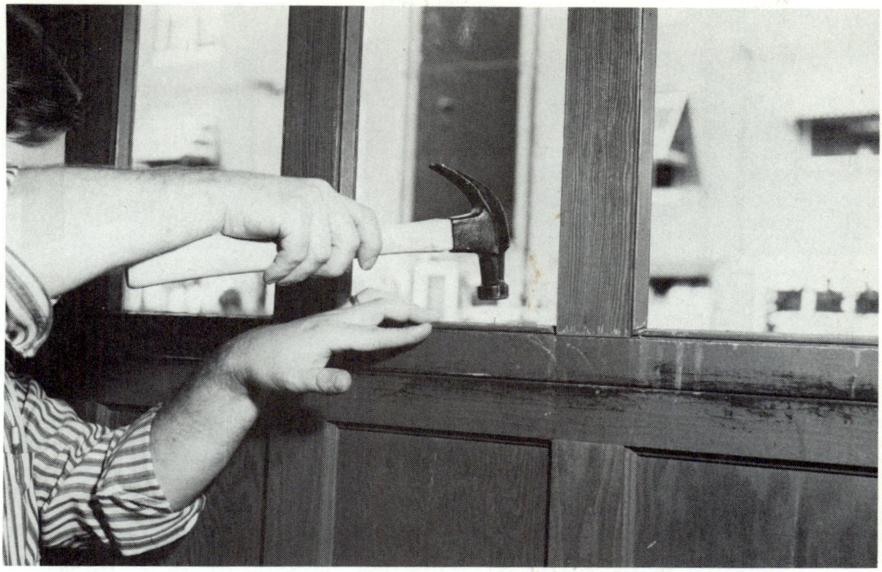

If you are using wood strips to hold plexiglass windowpane, replace them to complete installation. Clean with 1% solution of mild soap and water.

INSTALLING GLASS BLOCKS □ Glass block windows are a good replacement for tired old wood-framed basement windows, and any other window or opening with decorative functions that can be given up for greater home security. Installing such a window is somewhat more involved than working with acrylic.

The basic tools you'll need for installing glass blocks include a trowel, a level, a crowbar and hammer. To install a glass block window, first remove the old window, frame and all. Pack insulation between the facade and base wall, then remove all debris from the opening. Mix your mortar using one part cement to one part sand, plus water to the desired consistency. You may want the mortar to be somewhat stiffer than what you would use for laying conventional bricks.

If your home is new, you may want to install an expansion joint before beginning. Otherwise, the first course can be laid right in the old opening. Spread a layer of mortar, put in the blocks and level and align them. Then check your dimensions. Continue course by course, making sure to check dimensions and alignment after each course is completed. Let the mortar set five to ten minutes, then wash off the excess mortar with water and paper towels.

Installing Glass Block Windows

When installing glass block windows, use mortar made of one part cement to one part sand. Trim excess mortar off with trowel as each course is laid.

After mortar has set, wash off window with water and paper towel.

Your completed glass block window is hard to beat for security, energy saving and privacy.

WINDOW SHUTTERS □ Some experts predict that, because of its energy-saving advantages, the bona-fide window shutter which can be closed and opened at will is going to make a return. Such shutters help make your home more secure by making windows less accessible to burglars. If you can't find them on the market, you still have the option of constructing your own shutters.

Let's say you have a summer home with an outside sheeted with 1/2″ exterior plywood, and sliding aluminum windows. You could build your own shutters of 1/4″ exterior plywood, reinforced with a sturdy frame and vertical strips to simulate boards and bats.

Here's how one homeowner did it. He bolted each shutter—except those that were high enough to be inaccessible—on the inside with three bolts, one at the bottom center and one on each side. The tops were fastened with piano hinges. They thus serve a dual purpose as awnings and shutters.

When the home is occupied, the shutters are held open by one or two 5/16″ rods fastened to the top of the shutters by eyebolts. The rod bottoms are threaded and held in place by two nuts in a slotted,

Installing Window Shutters

Shutters can be constructed by the homeowner to boost security. Shutters (closed above) are 1/4" reinforced plywood; held open (right) by 5/16" cold rolled bar stock.

stainless steel clip which is screwed to the wood surrounding the window. The 3′×3′ windows require only one rod to hold them open, while larger windows either 3′×6′ or 4′×8′ require two rods to hold them open. When two rods are used, each is spaced one-fourth the length of the shutter from each end.

Since the aluminum windows are flush with the outside of the home, a way had to be devised to get the bolt between the sash and the inside of the shutter. This homeowner ripped 2′×6′ lumber in half to make frames that were spiked edgewise to the outside of the home around the windows. Then 16d spikes were used in holes drilled and counterbored in advance so the heads of the spikes and a piece of 5/16″ rod were inaccessible.

Because this method does not leave enough room to get hands between the sash (which is fixed in place) and the shutter, the homeowner made a rod long enough to extend out past the sash. To have enough wood to hold the bolt, he placed a strip of 5/8″ exterior plywood between the inside of the shutter and the 1″×2″ frame.

With conventional-type windows, you can adapt some method of fastening your shutters as required. Shutters not only make access difficult, but if your home is in a remote area, they discourage vandals and kids carrying firearms from shooting through windows, because they can't see them.

These are some relatively inexpensive steps you can take that are potentially effective in making windows more secure. More expensive, but also more effective, steps can be taken by incorporating windows into electronic security systems. The basics of these systems are outlined in Chapter 12.

How Shutters Work

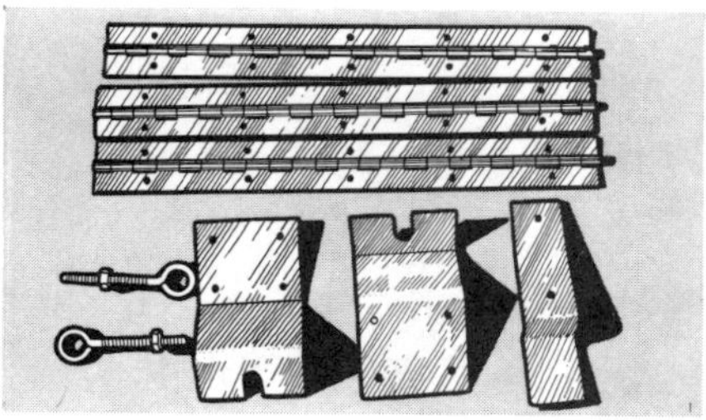

Hardware for each shutter includes three piano hinges, two eyebolts, two slotted support clips, one clip to hold rods out of way when not in use.

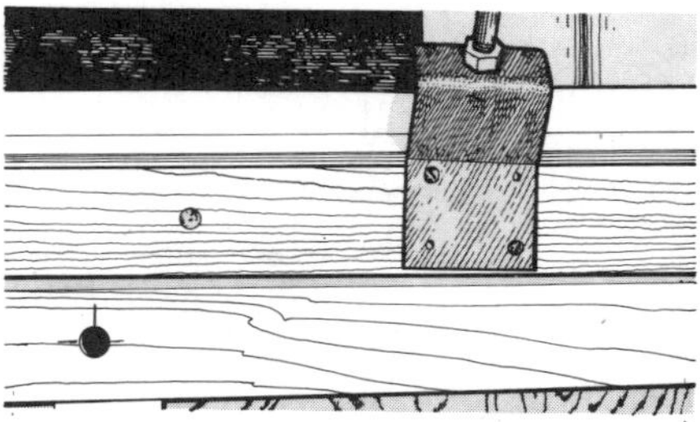

Support clip is screwed into sash and slotted to hold rods, which are held in place by two nuts. The 3′ windows require only one rod; larger windows need two.

Framework inside shutter is shimmed with 5/8″ plywood to make it thick enough to hold bolts used to fasten shutter when it is closed for season.

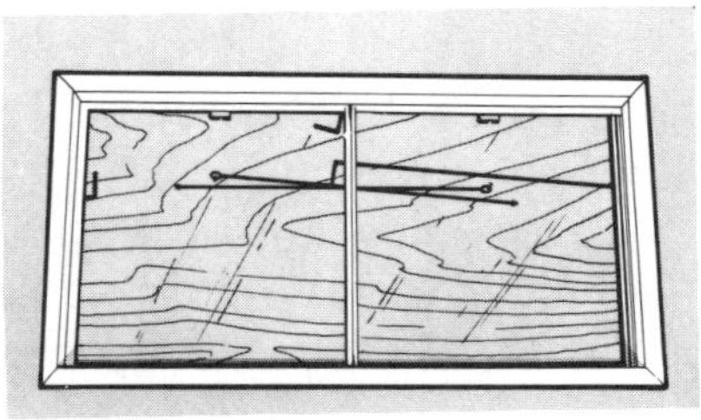

Support rods are held with metal clip inside closed and bolted shutters. Larger windows require two rods, while smaller windows need only one. They fasten at top with eyebolts.

How to Mark Possessions

CHAPTER 6 ■ The rate of home burglaries has been reduced dramatically in many areas with the use of simple, inexpensive methods of marking valuables.

The plan works like this: You engrave an identifying number on items that burglars find most appealing—radios, stereos, TV sets, tape recorders, cameras, bicycles, tools, typewriters, jewelry, musical instruments—and record the numbers. Then you put stickers on your home's front door or other highly visible place advising potential thieves that all items of value on your premises have been marked for ready identification by law-enforcement agencies.

This helps foil a thief in three ways. First, if he is stopped by police with the marked items in his possession, he can't plead convincingly that they are his own. Second, your possessions now are easily identifiable, which means that fences (middlemen who buy and resell stolen property) are cool toward the items; the thief gets stuck with the goods when what he really wants is money. Third, the stickers may discourage thieves from breaking in at all.

IDENTIFICATION PROGRAMS

■ Some communities that have instituted identification programs such as Operation Identification have experienced drastic reductions in residential burglaries. The idea began in Monterey Park, California, in 1963 when homeowners responded to a police department circular and began engraving numbers on their possessions to identify them if stolen. The result was that over a specific period of time only three bur-

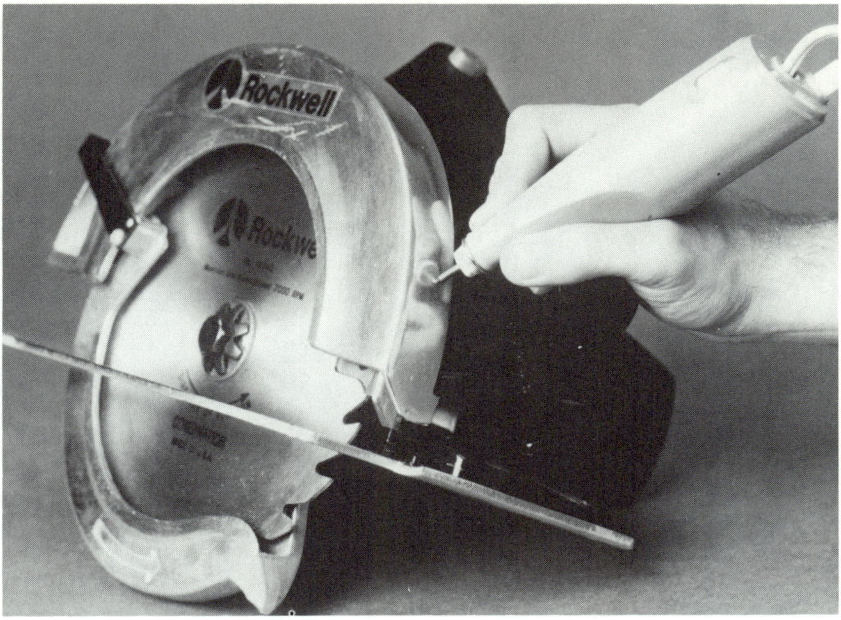

Some towns have had dramatic reductions in home burglaries after instituting possession-marking programs.

glaries occurred in 4,000 participating households. By contrast, over 1,800 burglaries were committed in 7,000 households that did not participate in the program.

Today the Independent Insurance Agents of America (IIAA), the National Sheriff's Association and many local police departments encourage homeowners to mark their personal possessions. An electric engraver pen is used to mark metal, wood and plastic objects with an identifying number that can't be obliterated. On metal, even if the numbers are filed down by a thief, they can be restored in police laboratories by a chemical process that makes them stand out clearly. Invisible ink can also be used.

Law-enforcement agencies may vary in their recommendations for the numbers to use. Some may issue you a computer-generated number which can be read by federal- and state-operated computerized crime-information systems, such as the FBI's National Crime Information Center. Others may suggest that you use your driver's license number or your telephone number. These numbers are easily

Warning labels for doors and windows are supplied by community programs, and by marketers of identification equipment.

Brinks labels come with invisible-ink felt-tip pen from Sanford Corp.

Other Brinks labels come with Dremel electric engraver.

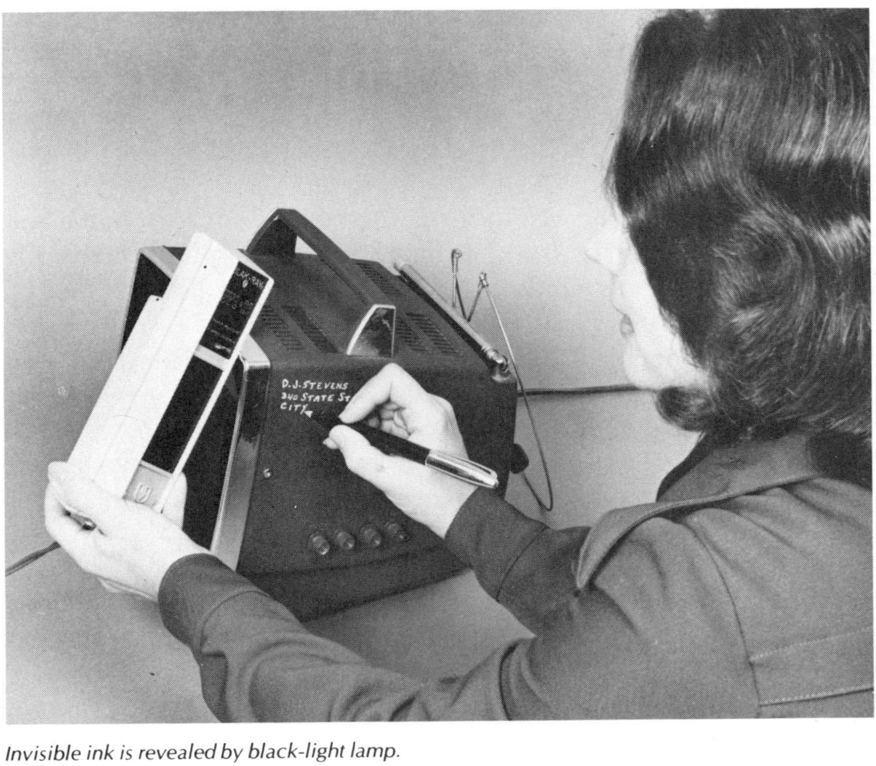

Invisible ink is revealed by black-light lamp.

Closeup shows engraved numbers on camera tripod.

recognizable and will immediately be traced to you. If you use your Social Security number you must also file this with the police, since federal law prohibits the use of a Social Security number to trace a person.

In New York City, police give two cards to participants in one identification program. On them they write their Social Security number followed by the letters NYC, their name, address, home and business phones. Participants are then given decals or printed labels that can be pasted on windows and doors. The decals state that all items of value on the premises have been marked.

Some police departments (and some insurance agents) will lend you an electric engraver for marking. They may also give you an inventory sheet on which to list all property you have marked and where the number is located on each item. You can buy your own marking equipment (see Appendix for sources), and you can use the inventory sheet on page 73 to list the property you mark.

The inventory sheet lists valuables that are most commonly the target of thieves. Put your identifying number near the manufacturer's serial number. Don't put the number on removable parts such as doors, lids and plates. Once you complete the form, store it in a safe place. If you should become the victim of a burglary, you can present the form to your local law-enforcement authorities and indicate which items were stolen. By doing this, you'll greatly boost your chances of having your property recovered.

MARKED POSSESSION INVENTORY

Items	*Mfr. Serial No.*	*Where Marked*
Adding Machines		
Appliances		
Battery Chargers		
Bicycles		
Binoculars		
Cameras		
Clocks		
Fishing Equipment		
Golf Clubs		
Jewelry		
Lawn Mowers (Power)		
Musical Instruments		
Photography Equipment (Projectors, Enlargers)		
Power Tools		
Radios		
Record Players, Stereos		
Small Hand Tools		
Sporting Goods		
Tape Recorders		
Televisions		
Typewriters		

All items on this form are marked with the following identifying number:

If you want a more precise inventory, you can make up your own form, as shown below, which includes description and/or brand name, plus the purchase date and price.

Item	*Description/Brand Name*	*Serial No./OPID No.*	*Purchase Date/Price*
Color TV	23″ Zenith Table Model	1001100/Mo.33383383	December 1978/$565
B/W TV	17″ RCA Portable	RCA345678/Mo.33383383	June 1978/$195
AM-FM Radio	Panasonic Table Model	JA79T34B/Mo.33383383	March 1971/$70
Tape Deck	Teac Reel to Reel	T-34589/Mo.33383383	August 1975/$375
35mm Camera	Nikon FTN	7203841/Mo.33383383	May 1972/$585

It's a good idea to take a photograph of items that are not marked with serial numbers or identifying numbers. If you store your inventory sheet in a place other than at home, you may want to keep an extra copy for convenient reference and updating.

EQUIPMENT FOR MARKING

ELECTRIC ENGRAVERS □ These are simple tools which can be plugged into any electric outlet. They have hardened carbide-steel or diamond tips, and are about 6″ to 7″ long. The point moves at very high speed, making a groove in the material. You write with it as if it were a ball point pen. You can buy your own for about $15 at a hardware store or anyplace electric tools are sold.

INVISIBLE INK □ There are some items that would be defaced or ruined by an electric engraver—antiques, fine china, silverware, paintings, fur garments, negotiable securities. Police and IIAA agents recommend using invisible ink on these items. Numbers written in this ink are clearly revealed under black-light lamps which give off ultraviolet rays, used by police departments with crime prevention sections.

Identifying numbers should be written on the backs of fine furs (under the lining), on the reverse side of paintings and in inconspicuous places on antiques. TV sets and other electronic equipment can be marked almost anywhere since the ink cannot be seen.

You may have difficulty locating an invisible-ink marker. They look like a black pen with a white felt tip. Some stationery and hardware stores carry them, as do some locksmiths.

SCRIBERS □ If an electric engraver is unavailable, you can use a scriber, which is simply a steel marking tool used in carpentry. Scribers have a hardened steel point with a carbide-steel or diamond-point tip. They are available in many hardware stores. Scribers are not as efficient on metal as electric engravers, but if you press down firmly you can scratch a number plainly enough to help the police identify your property. Some companies sell devices that etch marks on metal with acid.

COMMUNITY PROGRAMS

■ If you want to start a community-wide identification program, first check with local police, then write to: Independent Insurance Agents of America, c/o Operation Identification, 85 John St., New York, NY 10038.

Many communities have organized neighborhood crime watches designed to support the identification programs. These watches are simply groups of neighbors who agree to keep an eye on each other's homes and immediately report suspicious activity to police. This is a good way to increase cooperation between community residents and police.

As long as burglars have a choice between marked and unmarked property, you owe it to yourself to take action. On a burglar's rating scale, you want to be as close to the bottom of the heap as you can possibly get.

Using Light to Your Advantage

CHAPTER 7 ■ Darkness offers concealment, and from a concealed position a burglar can take his time with the job. Any light source—even a full moon—acts as a deterrent to the burglar who works at night. It's a lot easier for a thief to get past your door locks if it's dark and he can take his time without fear of being noticed.

Home lighting reduces burglary rates. The Law Enforcement Assistance Administration of the U.S. Department of Justice has researched it; so have Westinghouse, General Electric and a number of state and local governments. The $120 million being spent each year on security lighting shows that homeowners are becoming aware of its value. The evidence indicates that lighting—properly placed and timed—can protect your home from prowlers and increase nighttime safety for you, your family and legitimate visitors.

INTERIOR LIGHTING

■ To help decoy burglars into thinking someone is at home, you can leave interior lights on while you are away. The light you leave on should not necessarily be the lamp in the front window; lights in one or two interior rooms are a good idea. A better bet, however, is to buy one or more lighting timers which turn lights on and off in different rooms at designated times.

You can generally buy a good timer for $10 or less. Three or four individual timers can do a good job of simulating an occupied home. For example, you can use one timer in the kitchen which turns lights on at 7 P.M. and off at 11 P.M. A

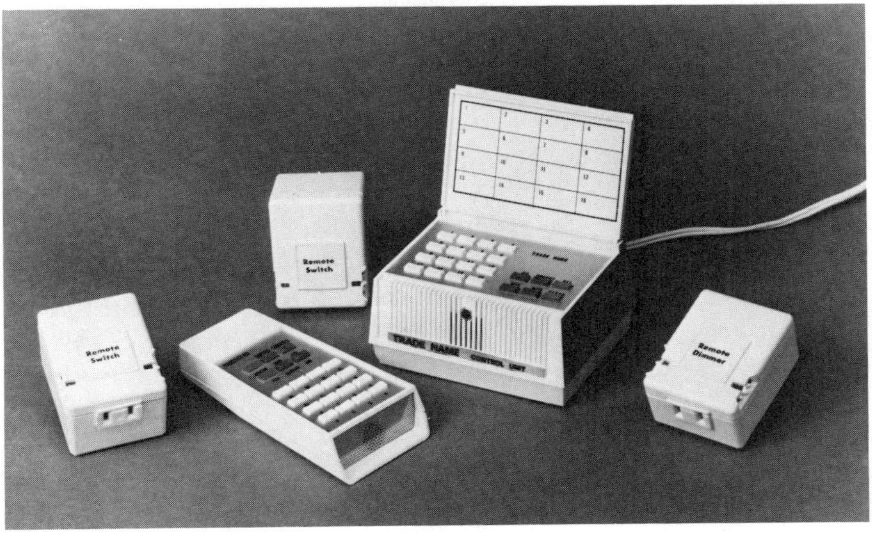

This home electrical control system makes it possible to turn lights and appliances on and off from central control box. Further adaptations, which will be available soon, will let you preprogram lighting throughout your home to decoy burglars while you are away.

second timer can be used in the living room to turn lights on at 8 P.M. and off again at midnight. A third timer can be used in the bedroom, set to turn lights on at midnight and off at 1 A.M. A fourth timer can be set to turn a light on in the bathroom at midnight, and off again in the morning.

You can alter the hours, but the main idea is to re-create your normal living schedule. Timers can also be used to turn appliances such as TVs and stereos off and on.

Besides individual timers, new equipment is coming on the market that further simulates an occupied home. It is expected that future systems will have the capacity to be programmed so that electricity can be fed automatically to lights and appliances throughout the home in any predetermined sequence.

One inexpensive electrical control system is now available from Sears. It uses a central switching console along with special lamp and appliance modules that enable you to turn electricity on and off both inside and outside the house, whether you're at home or not. With this system, you can alarm an intruder by turning on all inside and outside lights with the touch of a single button, or you can light remote areas of your home before entering.

The system includes a 16-switch command console which plugs into a wall outlet and transmits coded signals over the home's electrical wiring system to lamp, appliance and wall-switch modules. A lamp module receives the signal to turn on or off, or to dim or brighten. The module plugs into a wall outlet and a lamp plugs into the module. Appliance modules work in the same way, but they handle appliances that use up to 15 amps. You can install wall-switch modules as you would conventional wall dimmers. They receive coded signals from the command console to control those lights normally operated by a wall switch, such as outside, garage and ceiling lights.

The command console runs about $40, while the wall-switch module sells for about $15, the lamp module for about $14 and the appliance module for about $15. Select from these components to put together a system designed to best fit your needs.

EXTERIOR LIGHTING

■ Lighting installed around home entranceways, paths and walks, steps, garages and recreational areas will help deter prowlers and vandals. Following is what experts on lighting recommend. Use the help of a licensed electrician to choose appropriate fixtures and to make sure systems are wired in compliance with safety codes.

ENTRANCEWAYS □ Incandescent lamps from 25-watt decorative types to 150-watt PAR (incandescent reflector) lamps are often used. Newer mercury lamps in the 50- to 175-watt size range can also be considered. Wall-mounted brackets in pairs are usually preferred, one on either side of the door. An effective mounting location is 5½′ above standing level. A single fixture, at the same height, is best located on the lock side of the door or centered above the door.

Good alternatives for entranceways are recessed units in the ceiling or the roof overhang. Fixtures mounted higher than standing level require higher-wattage lamps. At least 60 watts are recommended for side brackets, while 75- or 100-watt lamps are recommended for above-the-door fixtures. To keep lights from being offensively bright at night, shielding or diffusing glass can be used.

STEPS, PATHS AND WALKS □ The same types of lamps and

How to Light a Home's Exterior

"Moonlight" fixture in tree is shielded by 24" length of 6"-diameter stovepipe and equipped with weatherproof socket and 100-watt PAR lamp. Decorative planter lights at corner of garage illuminate walk entrance into driveway.

A spread-lens fixture suspended from and concealed by tree branches distributes light along with 60-watt lamp in mushroom unit, which lights steps. Bulb is shielded from view.

Two 40-watt lamps in pair of prismatic glass brackets are 5½′ above driveway and are on high-low switch circuit. Lighted house number at room peak uses low-voltage lamps connected to bell transformer.

wattages can work. You can get several types of equipment for mounting lamps below eye level in order to light ground areas. Ground-spike units and units with louver or lens-plate light distribution can be installed in walls next to paths or walks. Overhead units are also available for in-tree or pole mounting. Post-top and wall-mounting lanterns designed for both decorative style and functional lighting are also available.

Ground-lighting units which are installed below eye level normally light no more than an 8′-diameter area, and coverage is influenced by the size and shape of the reflector used. Generally, complete shielding of below-eye-level light sources is needed to keep from

Two 12v PAR-56 wide floodlamps are recessed in sides of pool. Highlights on trees are from 100-watt clear mercury floods and 150-watt PAR floods.

Here is an example of a lighted garden fixture that deters unwelcome guests and adds to nighttime safety. Easily constructed by the home handyman, unit uses globe-shaped bulb that is weatherproof and shatterproof.

Another garden fixture using bulbs in brass base that will not corrode or freeze in socket.

blinding your guests and family. When using light alongside stairs, pay particular attention to shielding because of the low viewing angles.

Space ground-lighting units so that semidark spaces between the pools of light are not greater than the width of the light pools. Louvered or lens-plate equipment installed in walls adjoining paths are effective mounted between 16″ and 24″ above the ground, and not more than 8′ apart. They work well when recessed into stair risers.

Post lanterns are effective lighting tools provided they are not glaringly bright or restrictive in distributing light. Overhead floodlighting from poles 10′ to 20′ high offer the advantage of widespread light distribution or sharp spot-beam control. Floodlighting lamps are effective in shields at least 9″ deep, which hide the direct brightness of the lamps. Low-voltage lamps are another choice; they have built-in shielding that inhibits spill light, thus controlling excessive brightness.

GARAGES AND PARKING AREAS □ Plan lighting to eliminate between-car shadows. This will make access to cars easier and cut down on hiding places for vandals. Lamps of 75 to 100 watts are usually adequate for small parking places. Larger areas can be lighted with low-wattage mercury lamps or fluorescent units. Inside garages, 75- or 100-watt incandescent lamps or 40-watt fluorescents are adequate.

Bare lamp fixtures are suitable for brief-period convenience lighting in garages. But fixtures with some light-source shielding add visual comfort. When possible, locate ceiling-mounted lighting units so people getting in and out of cars don't step out into car-door shadows. Locate ceiling fixtures about 6′ back from the front-bumper plane of the parked car. Place them above between-car walk spaces rather than over car stalls.

Lighting for garage entrances is effective when installed 5½′ above standing level and on both sides of the door. You can also use overhead lighting set into the roof overhang, with one unit centered over a single garage door.

POOLS □ Regular-voltage or low-voltage PAR floodlights cannot be closer than 5′ to a pool, according to the National Electrical Code. For underwater lighting, 12v lamps available in 300- to 500-watt sizes can be used. A ground fault interrupter will help ensure electrical safety.

For floodlighting around the pool, deep-shielded bullet-type fixtures are effective mounted 20′ or less above the ground in trees, on poles or on fence tops. The rule of thumb for spacing between units is no more than twice the distance above the ground—10′ apart, for instance, at the top of a 5′-high fence.

PATIOS AND OTHER OUTDOOR AREAS □ You can use a 150-watt PAR-38 floodlamp 15′ above the patio and aim in at a 45° angle to light a 55′×30′ area. To light a wider area, try double floodlights that swing in two directions from one base. Fluorescents can be used to give a patio the feeling of an outdoor "room." But to operate fluorescents at temperatures of 32°F or below, special ballasts and fixtures are necessary. Also, for general winter use, a special covering is needed. For a unique patio lighting effect, string up 25-watt globe-type bulbs with their rubber sockets about 24″ apart.

A word about bulbs. A bulb that will be exposed to wind and rain should be weatherproof and shatterproof. If an outdoor fixture will house the bulb, you can use energy-saving light bulbs and economize on your electrical bill. Some energy-saving incandescent bulbs on the market offer the same amount of light as conventional bulbs, but use less electricity and last longer. If you choose PARs, a weatherproof bulb is needed if the floodlight holder shields the lamp base only. If the fixture fully shields the bulb, you can use an indoor bulb.

Outdoor lights can be hooked up to a photoelectric eye that turns them on at dusk and off at dawn. You can buy an adapter that screws into the socket to do this. You can also buy special outdoor security lights that have built-in photo control. A photo cell automatically turns the light on and off, or can be controlled manually with a switch.

One such unit, from Edison Lighting, comes with everything you need to install it quickly and easily on a wall or pole. A prewired socket runs on standard house current. The unit's 175-watt white mercury lamp is said to last 12 times longer than a 150-watt PAR lamp. The following chart is used to help determine mounting height.

ILLUMINATED CIRCLE/MOUNTING HEIGHT GUIDE

Mounting Height:	15′	18′	20′	25′	30′	35′
Illuminated Circle Diameter:	80′	100′	110′	140′	165′	190′

LOW-VOLTAGE SYSTEMS □ Safe, economical to operate and easy to install, weatherproof low-voltage outdoor lighting systems let you add to home security as well as bring instant beauty to the home landscape. Spotlights, for example, can be used to splash light of different hues about your house and yard. Area lights can shed a festive glow around patios and along walkways to make after-dark entertaining a pleasure.

Modern low-voltage outdoor lighting systems operate on 12 volts, rather than the 120 volts the power line delivers. This makes low-voltage lighting safe and also makes installation feasible by the do-it-yourselfer. A 120v outdoor system falls under regulation of your local municipal electrical code. All 120v outdoor components and wiring must be in compliance with local codes, buried well below the ground surface. Municipal electrical inspection may be required.

With 12v lighting systems, the restrictions are reduced. The power to operate the lights is furnished by a step-down transformer that isolates the lighting line and fixtures from the lethal power line. Shock hazard, always a factor where power-line-operated devices are used outdoors, is virtually reduced to zero. Children and pets and people who are careless with power mowers have much less to fear from low-voltage systems.

There's another plus, too. Each 12v lamp in a typical system requires only 18 watts of power. This means that you can run six 12v lamps for about the same price you'd pay to run just one 120v spotlight.

Low-voltage outdoor lighting systems may use automotive-type bulbs in tough reflectorized enclosures, or sealed-beam lamps similar to those used in car headlights. The lamps are mounted in plastic housing of two kinds: 1) upright spots with push-in ground stakes to hold the light erect, and 2) mushroom fixtures in which the light shines up against a translucent or reflective dome that sheds even area illumination on pathways or plantings. Wall and post mounting is also possible for added flexibility in setting up a lighting scheme.

Systems are sold with a certain number of lights that total a power consumption within the rated capacity of the transformer. Generally there is enough capacity to handle one or two additional lights, and many manufacturers supply these as accessories.

Lamps feature clip-on connectors that use two insulation-piercing points and a screw-on fitting. The connector is simply placed over the two-wire 12v line from the system transformer, then screwed down until the two piercing points bite into the supply wires. This simple connection method makes for quick hookup when you've found the right location for a light, or rapid relocation if you're not satisfied with the effect of your first try. There's no need to patch the tiny holes left in the cable if a connection is moved.

Most low-voltage lighting systems include a secondary supply line 100′ long, plus 25′-long cables on each lamp. This combination provides considerable flexibility.

The weatherproof transformer is usually installed in a protected location such as a corner or behind stonework, where it's difficult to bump with a power mower. The power cable attached to the transformer should be plugged into a nearby weatherproof outlet.

Note: Don't use extension cords. They can be lethal outdoors, and they are in violation of almost every electrical code for permanent use in an outdoor circuit. Play it safe and install, or have an electrician install for you, an outdoor 120v outlet to feed your low-voltage lighting system.

The average household 120v circuit is fused at 15 amperes. This means that its capacity is 1,800 watts. To see if an existing outdoor outlet circuit will handle your lighting and other outdoor needs, add up the wattage of all lights, motors, pumps, etc. that will be used at one time on the line. If the total is more than 1,800, a separate circuit should be run from the house main panel.

Underground 120v wiring offers maximum safety and convenience. Wire of types USE or UF can now be used underground without being enclosed in conduit or lead sheath. Either type of cable should be buried at least 12″ deep as protection against accidental severing by groundbreaking tools and equipment. If the electric cable cannot be buried this deep, it should be fastened with cable straps to the underside of 1″×4″ redwood boards. The boards will act as a protective covering.

Where it emerges from underground, the cable must be protected by conduit or greenfield secured to a post. On top of the post is an aboveground outlet which must, in all cases, be grounded. Weatherproof outlets should always be used. They can be installed on fences, posts, trees or buildings. You may also wish to have an inside switch for your system to use as dusk approaches. Alternatively, if your outlet is always "live," you can choose a lighting system in which the transformer housing also contains a time switch. This allows you to set adjustable levers to govern when your lighting system will be switched on and off.

For adequate protection against moisture and animals, mount the transformer or combined timer/transformer unit several feet above ground level. A simple bracket is used most often in commercial systems.

To install, uncoil the 12v supply cable, laying it flat on the ground to determine how far your system's lights can be located from the transformer site. Some systems have a single two-wire supply line, while others provide double two-wire lines with separate connectors at the transformer. The latter type places the transformer at the center of the system, offering somewhat easier layout of a lighting system to cover a front yard or to encircle a pool or patio.

Once the system wire is uncoiled and laid out, unwrap and lay out the two-wire cords of each lamp to be used in your system.

With the components laid out so you can see how much latitude your system affords, consider what lighting effect you want to achieve. If your idea is to illuminate trees or plantings with spotlights, you can use two major lighting methods—uplighting and downlighting—to make your property a dazzling spectacle.

In uplighting, one or more spots are staked in the ground below a tree and directed up into its leafy branches. This provides an ever-changing pattern of illumination and silhouetting as breezes stir the leaves. Downlighting of trees requires placing spots in upper branches so that the light shines down through the leaves to illuminate the ground below. Shifting patterns of color and shadows are projected onto the ground, providing an inviting, soft background.

Plantings can also be illuminated by colorful spots placed so the light source is not apparent. If you want to display your flowers, choose the color of the light with care. A red light will enhance roses, but the greens around it will show up a muddy brown. Green light is best for foliage, but may distort the hues of bright orange and red blossoms.

If your objective is to enjoy the natural beauty of your garden by night as you do by day, choose a white or bluish-white light, and splash colors elsewhere.

A pool or patio can be ringed with light by using mushroom lamps providing area downlighting. The soft, diffused light shed by these lamps can be augmented by spots illuminating features of interest. Try to avoid placement that subjects guests to the direct, harsh glare of a spot; reflective light is more congenial.

Falling water and colorful lighting are natural partners in creating a striking exterior decor. A fountain, waterfall or reflecting pool illuminated by spots or special underwater lamps becomes a scene of rippling, dynamic beauty. Glare is a principal enemy in this case. Place lights carefully, avoiding lighting angles that bounce annoying reflections back at the viewer.

Lighting of a house exterior must be planned with extra care to preserve the esthetic qualities of your home and still provide illumination to make it more secure. Low-key color, for example, can be added by area or walkway downlighting with mushroom lamps. Consider spots placed in soffits under the eaves or on nearby trees. These can shed soft downlight on lawn and plantings immediately forward of the house, creating a subdued reflection of color onto the house itself. The result is pleasing to the eye, yet you have made your home less attractive to potential thieves.

The Canine Approach

CHAPTER 8 ■ "Meaner than a junkyard dog." That observation in song recognizes a prime opportunity to boost home security.

Dog has served man as a basic home-security system since the beginning of time. If you have any doubt about how effective a good guard dog can be, ask your local junkman, gas station owner or police department.

A guard dog may be the best security system of all. One advantage to owning a dog trained to obey you and act as a guardian is the animal's ability to react intelligently. Another is that a dog is more personable than electronic equipment. Burglars can beat any system, even ultrasonic home-alarm systems. While dogs won't stop all thieves, it takes a determined burglar to get past a growling, snarling dog of any size.

Owning a dog is not all nirvana, of course. A dog used for security, like any other dog, must be walked, fed and otherwise cared for. And training is involved. You have to be willing to put in some effort, especially at the beginning.

A dog that's worth his salt can cost money. Besides maintenance costs, you may have to pay a fair amount for the animal if it's a purebred. Dogs for home security can generally be divided into three categories:

- Those that sound the alarm if someone tries to break into your home.
- Those that sound the alarm and pose a physical threat to the intruder.
- Those that are trained as attack dogs.

DISCRIMINATING BARKERS

■ Let's take a closer look. A dog sounds the alarm by barking. But the animal needn't be a St. Bernard or Great Dane to be effective. Most people can't tell the difference between the barking of large and small dogs. Even if an intruder can, he's likely to move on rather than break into a house where a dog is barking.

The idea is to train the dog so that it barks discriminately. You don't want a dog barking at everything. Exactly when you want a guard dog to bark is up to you. Some owners may want the dog to bark only at strange noises, while others may want it to sound the alarm if someone comes to the door.

In any case, training the dog is eased considerably by getting a dog that is prone to bark in the first place. The American Kennel Club

You don't have to have an attack dog to put up a sign like this, which may be enough to cause a thief to pick an easier target.

puts dogs into six groupings: sporting dogs, hounds, working dogs, terriers, toys and nonsporting dogs.

Dogs that are natural barkers are usually found among the working dogs. But terriers and toys also can work out well. From the working group, such dogs as Doberman pinschers, German shepherds, Rottweilers and Belgian sheepdogs are particularly good. Rated strictly for home security, the best are dogs from the working group, followed by terriers and toys.

Just because a dog is a particular breed is no guarantee that it will make a good guard dog—one that will bark and respond when someone approaches its territory. Even dogs within a particular breed have different temperaments. For example, 50 out of 100 German shepherds may be barkers that are protective, natural guard dogs. The rest may be too placid or too unruly. Some dog trainers prefer purebreds because they are more certain of what they'll get, but mutts may also work out at a much lower original investment.

You should structure a dog's barking. Teaching a dog to bark discriminately is not difficult. For example, you can have a helper approach a door or window silently while inside you whisper to the dog, "What's that? What's that?" The dog will bark, and should be congratulated with a "Good dog!"

Some trainers use a simple panel with buzzers, chimes and bells to train a dog to bark or not bark, depending on the sound activated. You can use your own front doorbell, buzzer or chimes in the same manner. Have somebody ring the bell. If your dog barks and you don't want him to, say "No!" After a while the dog will get the idea.

Guard dogs should be obedience-trained to heel, sit, go, etc. on command. It makes little sense to have a dog around and then have to put it down in the basement anytime you have a visitor.

Training is effective in terms of home security. If a criminal comes to your house posing as a meter reader and the dog charges him, it's psychologically effective when the dog stops dead on your command. A potential burglar will remember that.

If you want to teach your dog to bark discriminately and obey commands, your library can help. One good book is *The Guard Dog* by Gerald J. Mundis (David McKay, $8.95). To obedience-train a dog professionally can cost anywhere from $20 to $400, depending on the dog. But don't rush a dog into training—start when the dog is eight or nine months old and its changing hormones have had a chance to settle down.

A dog needn't be big to carry out the guard-and-alarm function successfully. Temperament is much more important than size for this purpose.

PHYSICAL THREATS

■ Dogs that both sound the alarm and pose a physical threat are the second kind of guard dog to consider. This type is not essentially different from the first type, except for size. When you own a large dog, word has a way of getting around. You walk the dog, it looks out a window, people know about it. And if one of these people happens to be a criminal, he'll overlook your house as an easy hit.

A large guard dog can also be psychologically comforting to the owner, even if its temperament would keep it from physically attacking an intruder. It can be reassuring to have a large dog padding around the house in the middle of the night or curled up at the foot of the bed. A large dog can also serve as a mobile security system. A criminal will think twice before accosting a woman in a car with a German shepherd sitting in the backseat.

What about the dangers of a large dog if you have young children? Kids being kids, the dog is bound to get some abuse. In general, females are better with children, while males make better watchdogs. The females will take more abuse. But there is a limit to what any dog will take. It's important to make any dog a member of the family, rather than to isolate it in a doghouse or in the yard. A dog that is allowed in the house and grows up with kids around will be less likely to bite anyone.

However, if you prefer to keep your dog outside, construct a kennel that will be good for the dog. Locate it close to the house; if your house is L-shaped, you can use two of its walls as kennel walls. Good basic material for kennel walls is chain-link fence in prefabricated sections. It can be made up in various heights and lengths and bolted together, and the posts don't have to be sunk in the ground, as with running chain-link fence. Wall height can vary from 4′ for small dogs to 6′ for larger ones.

The kennel should be at least 10′×10′ and contain a house big enough for the dog to stand up and turn around in. The house should not be much larger if the animal is to stay out there in cold weather, because the dog's body heat will be dissipated. Install a plastic or canvas flap over the entrance and a baffle (a small hallway leading to the entrance) to keep out bad weather.

ATTACK DOGS

■ What about attack dogs? Trainers prefer to call this type of dog "protection trained." Attack dogs vary in terms of when they will attack. Some are trained to attack on command, while those used to protect industrial establishments will attack any intruder automatically.

Generally it's not recommended that a homeowner buy an attack dog, simply because under normal circumstances it is not required.

How Attack Dogs Work

Attack dogs like this one cost $500 to train, but generally are not needed by the homeowner. Other types of guard dogs can serve the purpose equally well.

Attack dog appears to be like any other dog—warm, friendly and obedient.

As trainer approaches in suspicious manner, training begins to show.

Trained attack dog takes action by leaping at "intruder."

There is no particular problem to owning one as long as it has the right temperament and is properly trained. It's a must, however, for this type of dog to be professionally trained. It's expensive—around $500.

Whatever kind of dog you get, make sure it's healthy. It should not have mucus coming from its nose, nor should its eyes run. It should have an outgoing temperament and when you feel its flesh you should be able to discern fatty tissue.

"Intruder" is effectively deterred.

Detectors That Smell Trouble

CHAPTER 9 ■ You don't have to spend a bundle to disaster-proof your home. Five years ago it would have cost you thousands of dollars to equip your home with detectors to alert you and your family of fire, gas leaks, severe storms, power failure in critical appliances, or ground failure in electrical appliances. Right now, if you choose to bypass a complete home-security system package, $300 will still buy you immeasurable protection, including:

■ A couple of smoke detectors to save your life in case of fire.

■ A gas detector to monitor dangerous concentrations in your furnace or utility room.

■ A storm detector to warn your family of impending electrical storms and tornadoes.

■ A power failure detector to let you know immediately if power is lost to refrigerators, freezers, furnaces or greenhouses.

■ A number of ground fault interrupters that sense faults in electrical devices to protect you from the lethal dangers of electrical shock.

SMOKE DETECTORS

■ The advances in producing smoke detectors since their introduction in 1966 are dramatic. The first AC-powered models then sold for around $125, and battery-powered detectors introduced in the early 1970s cost more than $100. Because of volume and technological improvements, prices for smoke detectors have dropped drastically while their quality has im-

proved. Competition for sales has worked for the consumer, too. About 25 companies currently make smoke detectors, which are marketed under approximately 135 different names.

According to experts at the Center for Fire Research, National Bureau of Standards, about 80% of all fire deaths result from residential fires. Between 40% and 50% of all residential fire deaths could be avoided if all households were equipped with detectors.

Homeowners are buying detectors at an unbelievable rate. Sales in 1971 totaled 50,000 units. By 1977, 14 million were sold. Still, despite the high rate of sales, only about 12 million of the 80 million households in the U.S. were protected in 1978.

Some 33 states now have some sort of legislation requiring detectors in new construction. Most requirements for existing houses are legislated at local or county government levels. But agencies such as the National Bureau of Standards, the National Fire Protection Association, and those responsible for state and local fire codes say you are cheating yourself and your family if you don't have at least one smoke detector—and preferably one per floor—in your home.

If you're waiting for the price of smoke detectors to drop further, you may be disappointed. Prices are about as low as they will get, and it's a rare household that can't afford at least one effective smoke detector.

Many fire departments will survey your home and advise you on the best location for your detector. Chapter 10 explains in detail how to install a smoke detector. Briefly, some detectors wire directly into the electrical system. Others are battery powered. Some plug into outlets. Detectors react to the presence of smoke or fire by sounding a horn or buzzer. The alarm is triggered by either an ionization chamber or by photoelectric beam.

A considerable battle rages among makers of the two types of alarms, each side claiming superiority. The battle, say impartial observers, is regrettable since some bewildered homeowners may end up not buying either type of alarm. Experts say ionization detectors have a slight advantage with flaming fires; photoelectrics have a slight advantage with smoldering fires.

However, specialists at the National Fire Protection Association say there is no major difference between the two types in terms of escape time. The important things are that your home have at least one detector per floor, of either type, and that the detectors you buy have UL approval.

Some manufacturers are now offering alarms that have both ionization and photoelectric detectors. Such dual-alarm detectors have the best attributes of both types, and still cost less than $50.

GAS DETECTORS

■ Many homeowners fear gas leaks as much as the possibility of fire, in spite of the fact that 53 million U.S. homes use natural, liquified petroleum (LP) or propane gas. Several companies now offer alarms

GAS ALARM

Gas detectors used with LP gas should be positioned 6" to 12" above floor since LP gas is heavier than air.

that signal the presence of escaping gas. These can be used in houses, mobile homes, garages or apartments to warn residents before gas reaches flash-fire or explosive levels.

The major cause of gas leaks is a damaged or leaking gas line which permits gas to seep into the basement. Other causes include pilot lights going out; malfunctioning safety valves; and chimney, flue or furnace malfunctions that return gases to the home. Therefore, locations for gas alarms include the kitchen, and furnace, laundry and utility rooms.

Gas alarms have been around for some time, but often were so sensitive that false alarms frequently occurred. However, recently introduced gas alarms have minimized this problem. One newer unit on the market has a sensor that is heated to 250°F. When gas enters the chamber, solid state circuitry allows its presence to be analyzed. If gas buildup is sufficient to constitute a threat, a piercing alarm sounds.

Though standards for the installation of gas alarms have not been established, manufacturers recommend that they be put near the floor for heavier propane gas, at or near ceiling height for natural-

If natural gas is used, alarm should be 6" to 12" below ceiling since gas is lighter than air. These detectors mount in same way as smoke detectors (see Chapter 10).

gas protection. A typical unit's alarm will sound when room air has a .5% (propane) or 1% (natural gas) buildup. Explosive or flash-fire levels for propane gas are 2.2%; for natural gas, 5% or over.

Prices range from about $20 to $60. One word of caution: Don't be misled by companies trying to sell gas alarms as fire alarms. They will not work for fire detection. As with all detectors, use the UL listing as a guide to quality.

STORM DETECTORS

■ Tornadoes have been occurring with increasing frequency since the 1940s. Many climatologists believe it could be because weather patterns indicate a cyclical trend toward cooler conditions. April through July are the most active tornado months, with a peak in May of 140 tornadoes on the average. Most common in "tornado alley" —Texas up through North Dakota in the central U.S.—twisters appear with varying frequency in all states.

Advances in technology have helped put homeowners one up on bad weather. One detector now available monitors the electromagnetic field of approaching storms up to 30 miles away. When electrical cloud activity reaches a rate of 1,000 or more discharges per second, and 20 discharges of $^{1}/_{10}$ second or longer duration in one minute, lights and a buzzer indicate tornado activity. The battery-powered unit has two lights and a meter on the front panel. When a storm approaches, the green panel signals storm activity. A red light flashes if the storm is intense. If the storm approaches tornado severity, an audible alarm sounds and the meter reads "danger."

A valuable feature of such a detector is its portability. It is completely self-contained, and with an accessory antenna can be used in boats, mobile homes, campsites or airplanes. Such a unit costs about $60.

You can also buy small, inexpensive radios that are set to monitor the continuous weather information from the National Weather Service. The unit fits your pocket. Turned on, but with volume down, the radio will buzz if severe storms or tornadoes are forecast. You then turn up the volume to hear the full report. You also can turn the volume up for continuous weather broadcasts around the clock.

SEVERE STORM ALARM

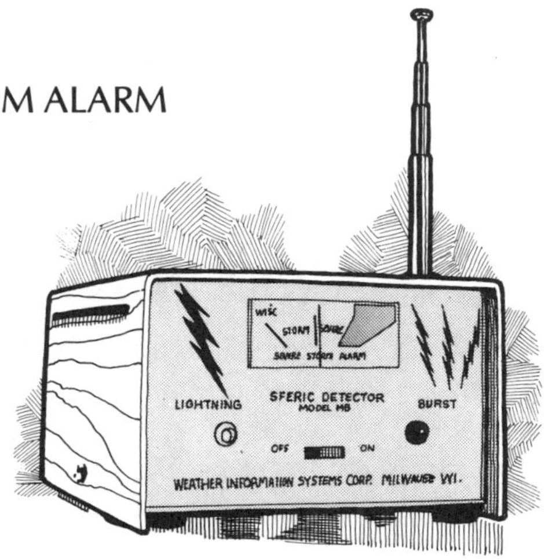

POWER FAILURE DETECTORS

■ These monitor power to freezers, sump pumps and other vital appliances or equipment to alert you to take action and avoid losses. When there is a total or circuit loss of power to critical appliances, such units give off an audible signal.

One plug-in alarm is powered by a 9v battery that has a four-hour life under continuous alarm indication. Plugged into a 110v outlet, the unit is self-deactivating when power is restored. It runs about $25.

You can also buy temperature alarms that fit through the doors of refrigerators or freezers. Such alarms warn you of malfunction or interrupted electricity supply when the temperature in the alarm unit rises above 20°F. One unit, which operates on a 9v battery, is available for $14.95.

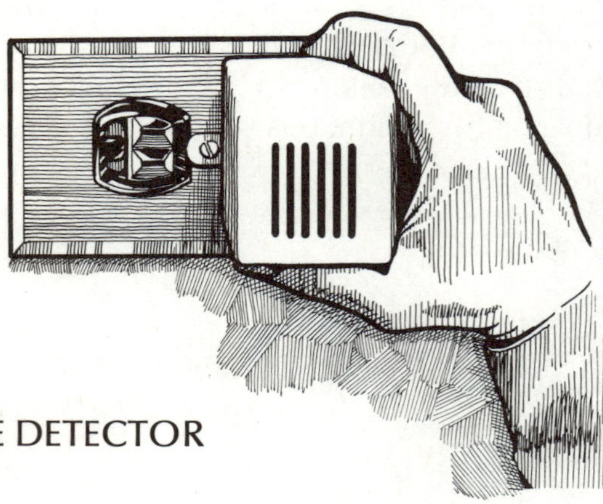

POWER FAILURE DETECTOR

GROUND FAULT INTERRUPTERS

■ These electrical devices are receiving wide endorsement by safety authorities and the National Electrical Code. Fuses and circuit breakers provide the basic fire protection in your home. They open the circuit if a faulty electrical device or an accidental short circuit causes whopping, heat-producing current to be drawn through the wires buried in your home's walls and ceilings. But fuses and circuit breakers don't provide any real protection to the guy who's holding a faulty power tool while standing in contact with the earth. A common fuse or breaker won't react until at least a 15-amp current

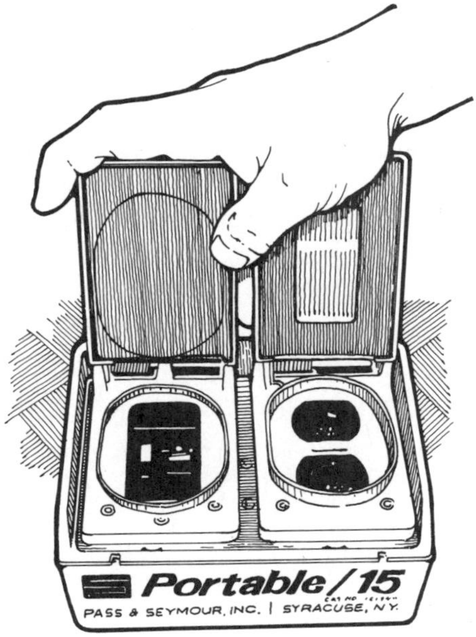

GROUND FAULT INTERRUPTER

is flowing—yet a human being can be electrocuted by only one-hundredth of that current!

Because three-wire mechanical grounding methods are not completely reliable, two new approaches to the problem have sprung up. First is double insulation, a method of building electrically powered tools and other devices so their electrical innards are completely insulated from metal parts liable to be contacted by the user; the entire device is enclosed in a nonconductive plastic housing. Second is an innovative safety unit that works with any electrical device, old or new, double-insulated or not—the ground fault interrupter, or GFI.

A GFI may be part of the electrical circuit-breaker box that supplies current to various outlets in your home. Or it may be a replacement wall outlet that fits in where the old outlet used to be. Or it may be a portable accessory that plugs in between a present outlet and the device you're using.

All GFIs work the same. They monitor the current flowing through the hot wire to a device, and the current flowing back through the neutral wire of the device. These currents are compared and should always be the same. If the current through the hot wire

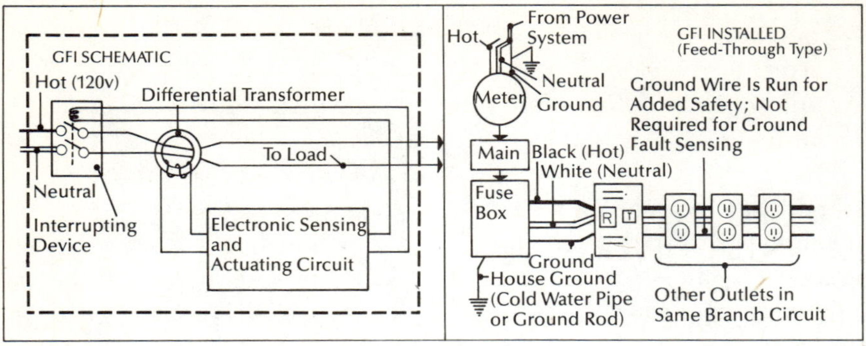

Power into GFI passes through contacts of interrupting device and through differential transformer. Currents through hot and neutral wires must be equal. If current through hot wire is greater, circuit trips interrupter before current reaches shock level. GFI installed as shown provides protection to several outlets in same branch circuit. In typical home power-distribution system it prevents hot wire from delivering 120 volts to grounded objects that are not stopped by fuse or circuit breaker.

exceeds the current through the neutral wire by as little as .005 amp, or 5 milliamperes (about one-thirtieth of the current it takes to light a flashlight bulb), the GFI immediately switches off power to the device it's serving.

Why? Because the GFI "knows" that any excess current is passing to ground via a pathway other than the neutral wire. That could mean a short or fault in the device you're using, and the path could be through your body to ground! The job of the GFI is to cut off current before it can reach the level where electrocution is possible. And it does so in 1/40 second—which is faster than you can blink your eyes!

There are three basic types of GFIs: circuit-breaker, wall-receptacle and portable. Here is a rundown on each.

CIRCUIT-BREAKER GFI □ If your home has a circuit-breaker box rather than an old-fashioned fuse box at the main power panel, this type of GFI can be used to replace the circuit breaker so the GFI circuit breaker is a dual-purpose unit that will break not only on large-scale overload currents as a conventional circuit breaker will, but on ground-fault currents too. This GFI can extend its ground-fault protection to any outlet served by the branch circuit fed through it.

However, incidental leakage current occurs in the best of home wiring systems. The longer the branch and the more devices it serves, the greater its leakage current. A circuit-breaker GFI senses this accumulated leakage, and so its operating tolerance is reduced. If normal leakage of the branch is 4 milliamperes and the GFI is set to trip out at 5, plugging in a device that has a slight leakage of 1 milliampere will cause the GFI to trip.

That can mean a long walk to the circuit-breaker box to reset the tripped GFI. It can also lead to disenchantment with the very real benefits of ground-fault protection. The right way to use a circuit-breaker GFI is to protect circuits that serve specific appliances such as swimming pool pumps, patio lights, etc. where the natural leakage of the branch is not so great that it will eat up the GFI's tolerance.

If you've recently added an electrical circuit to serve a swimming pool, bathroom or kitchen, you should use a circuit-breaker GFI to protect your family in these sensitive areas. Doing so means replacing an ordinary circuit breaker with a GFI that combines the fire-protection features of a circuit breaker with the protective features of a GFI.

Replacing a breaker with a GFI may require the services of a licensed electrician, depending upon the requirements of your local electrical code. However, the task involved is fairly simple. First, find the breaker that serves the electrical branch you want to protect. Note the physical dimensions and the current rating of the breaker. Stop by at your local electrical supply house and obtain a GFI-type breaker with the same current rating and installation dimensions. Install during daylight hours by turning off the main power switch, removing the standard breaker and mounting the GFI breaker in its place. Be sure to test after installation, following the GFI breaker manufacturer's recommendations.

WALL-RECEPTACLE GFI □ This protective unit is designed to replace a standard duplex receptacle in shop, kitchen, bathroom, garage or outdoors. It fits in a standard NEMA outlet box, and protects you against leakage currents from any device plugged into it.

An advantage of this type is that any natural leakage in the branch circuit leading to the GFI is ignored. This GFI type is convenient because it can be reset at the same location where it trips. And since it controls just one outlet rather than an entire branch circuit, its tripping won't plunge other sections of the house into darkness.

This GFI is the choice wherever you desire maximum protection in a limited area of electrical device use. It is easily installed because it takes the place of a standard outlet receptacle. And because this GFI is close at hand, not hidden away in a power box in the basement or garage, it is conveniently tested and reset.

Also available are feed-through receptacle GFIs. With this type, you gain not only protection at the receptacle you're replacing, but you can also extend this protection to other outlets downline of the GFI receptacle. To make this possible, a feed-through GFI receptacle has two extra terminals in addition to the normal three (hot, neutral and ground). These terminals are used to extend protected hot and neutral wires to the next outlets and fixtures in the branch.

To install a receptacle-type GFI, turn off power to the affected branch circuit by flipping the branch circuit breaker at the power box or by removing and pocketing the fuse. Next, remove the coverplate screw on the wall receptacle and lay the plate aside. Remove the two long screws that secure the duplex receptacle and pull the receptacle outward, loosening its terminal screws and freeing it from the hot, neutral and ground wires.

If the GFI you're installing is a three-wire type, simply connect hot (black), neutral (white) and ground (green or bare) wires to the appropriate terminals, following the manufacturer's diagram. This type will protect only devices that plug into its outlet. Install it in the box, taking care to dress the wires carefully, and replace the cover plate. Test as recommended by the manufacturer.

If the GFI you're installing is a feed-through type and you have determined that everything downline is fed through this circuit, connect the feed-line hot, neutral and ground to the GFI. Then connect the GFI's protected hot and neutral feed-through wires to the respective wires that feed the downline branch circuit.

Because of the extra wiring, feed-through GFIs tend to be somewhat bulkier than straight three-wire types. You may find it a tight squeeze to get the wiring, connectors and other components back into a snug outlet box. Some manufacturers solve this problem by offering standoff faceplates that bulge the GFI outward from the wall to give space behind the GFI for the extra wiring bulk.

PORTABLE GFI □ If you don't have dedicated GFIs (those that serve specific appliances) protecting outdoor, basement or garage outlets in your home, a portable GFI is a sensible investment for use with electrically powered tools in these areas, where your body is so likely to contact ground. Portables come in several forms. The simplest is a molded case with a three-prong plug on its back. You plug it into an outlet, then plug the device you'll be using into the protected receptacle on the front of the case.

Slightly different are the extension types. With these, an extension power cord plugs into an outlet at one end while the GFI is located at the other end, its receptacle feeding the device you're using. These GFIs are especially well suited for outdoor power tools such as electric lawn mowers, chain saws, tillers and hedge trimmers, as well as electric drills and saws. Portables feature all the test and indicating features of built-ins, but have the great advantage of going wherever you need their protection.

TESTING GFIs □ By testing any GFI once every month, you will know that you have working protection against accidental ground fault in sensitive areas in and around your home. In the very rare instance where the GFI does not test out, you will have detected a fault in it before it has been subjected to the crucial test of an actual ground fault where you might have been part of the electrical circuit.

Fire Defense System

CHAPTER 10 ■ Each year about 6,500 people die from fires and fire-related burns and accidents; of these, about 80% die at home. About 60% of all fatal household fires occur between 10 P.M. and 6 A.M., when most people are sleeping. The majority of deaths due to fires are not actually caused by heat or flames, but rather from the smoke and toxic gases of combustion. Many victims die in their sleep, never realizing that a fire was in progress.

For a small investment of time and money, you can greatly reduce the threat of fire by preparing your home, yourself and your family. Fires can be prevented. In fact, a recent government study shows that as many as 3,000 home fire fatalities could be avoided each year if good preventive measures were used. Many fire disasters can be avoided by simple, inexpensive installation of a fire-protection system.

Fires in homes can result from a variety of causes. Among the most frequent are carelessness in smoking habits, cooking and use of equipment such as gas stoves and tanks; faulty electrical wiring; children playing with matches; and improper storage of flammable liquids.

HOMEOWNER'S CHECKLIST

■ To avoid the hazard of fire, first make a checklist of possible hazards in your home and make sure they are taken care of immediately. Equip your home with inexpensive fire-protection equipment such as smoke detectors, extinguishers and escape ladders. Then sit down with your family and plan out an escape route for everyone, and make sure they all know it well enough to find it in the dark at night.

Following is a list of sound basic practices from the New York City Fire Department to help you avoid situations that can lead to fire in your home.

1. Keep noncombustible ashtrays in all rooms.
2. Carefully dispose of glowing matches and cigarettes.
3. Keep matches in metal containers away from heat and children.
4. Warn everyone in your family against smoking in bed.
5. Avoid running electric cords under rugs and over nails and hooks.
6. Keep lamp and appliance cords in good condition.
7. Limit the number of lights and appliances on each circuit. If fuses blow, you are probably overloading circuits. Solution: Relocate appliances or have additional circuits installed by a reliable electrician.
8. Purchase only UL-listed appliances.
9. Use only 15-amp fuses on lighting circuits.
10. Use only nonflammable cleaning fluids—check the labels.
11. Keep any necessary, flammable liquids in closed containers and use in properly ventilated areas. Use only approved safety cans for gasoline.
12. Keep your basement, storerooms and attic free from rubbish, oily rags and old papers.
13. If you use an old mop, keep it in a metal container in a well-ventilated place where it will not catch fire by spontaneous ignition.
14. Keep smoldering ashes in hole-free, covered metal containers.

INSTALLING SMOKE DETECTORS

■ **A reliable smoke detector will wake you and give you and your** family time to leave the house before it's too late. As was mentioned in Chapter 9, detectors use an ionization chamber, a photoelectric beam or a combination of the two to detect smoke. Some newer detectors have a light to orient people in a smoky hallway or room. They may be purchased and installed as individual units, or they can be tied into more sophisticated electronic security systems, as explained in Chapter 12.

Where to Put Smoke Detectors

GOOD: Install a smoke detector between sleeping areas and the rest of the house, and on each level of multilevel homes.

BETTER: Add additional detectors to the head of each stairway to occupied areas, and at the bottom of basement stairway.

BEST: Add detectors to living room, family room, basement or workshop, utility room, furnace room and each bedroom.

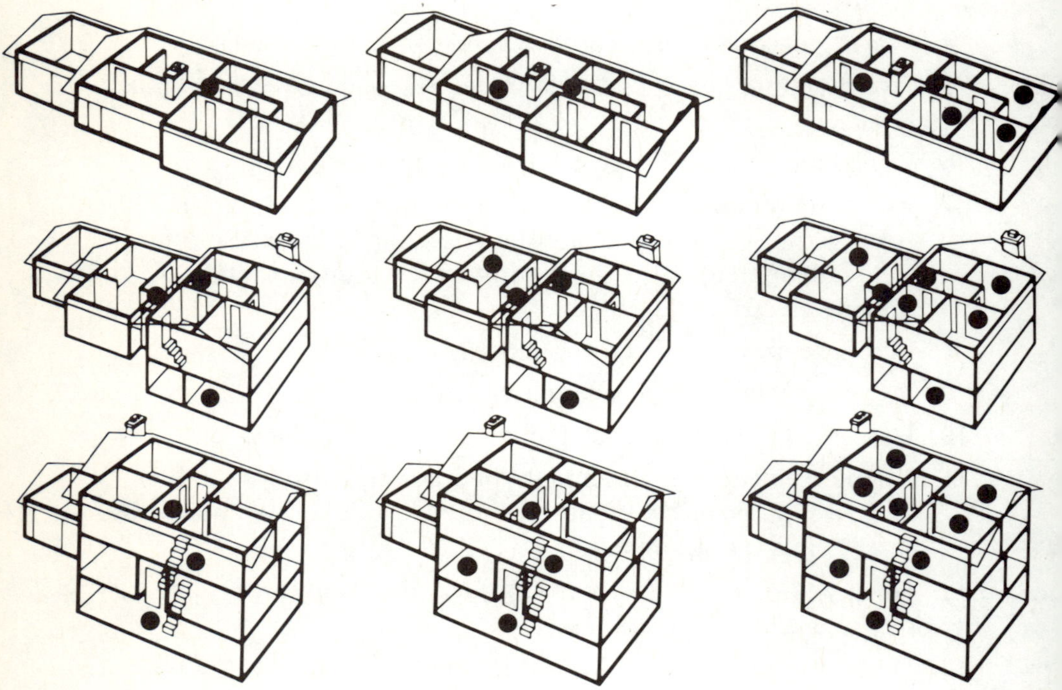

Because smoke rises, the best place to install a detector is on the ceiling or high on an inside wall just below the ceiling. However, if the ceiling is below an uninsulated attic or in a mobile home, the detector should be placed on the wall 4″ to 12″ below the ceiling. In a multilevel air-conditioned home, a detector is needed on each story. On the first floor, the detector should be placed on the ceiling at the base of the stairwell and/or in the living room. For basements, locate the detector on the ceiling at the bottom of the stairway.

Detectors should be installed close enough to bedrooms so the alarm can be heard if the doors are closed. Do not install one within

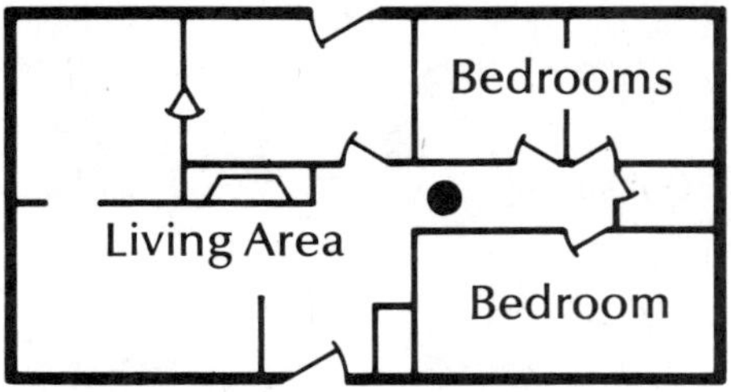

Locate smoke detector between sleeping and living areas if you have one bedroom area on one level.

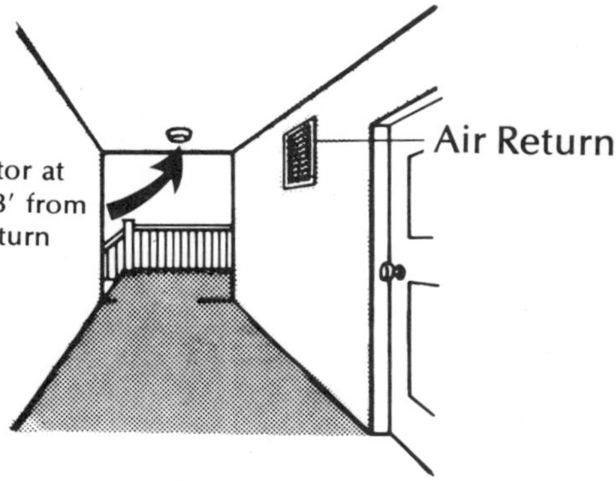

Avoid installing a smoke detector less than 3′ from an air-supply register that might blow smoke away from the detector.

3′ of an air-supply register that might blow the smoke away from the detector. A detector should not be installed between the air return to the furnace and the sleeping area; the smoke will be recirculated and diluted, resulting in a delayed alarm. If you usually sleep with your door closed, you might consider installing an additional detector inside the bedroom. If a fire starts in the bedroom, the detector inside that room will respond faster than the one in the hallway.

If you are sleeping, it may be difficult to hear a detector located away from the bedroom area. If you are installing more than one detector, consider purchasing units that can be interconnected. That way, when one unit detects smoke, all detectors will sound an alarm. They can be connected two ways: by pulling wires through the walls or by a wireless system. Pulling the wires through the walls is a more permanent method and may require the services of an electrician. The wireless system operates on the same principle as home wireless intercoms. Either procedure is effective.

Detectors are powered two ways: by batteries or by household electric current. Battery-operated detectors are the easiest to install. They require no outlets or connections to household wiring. However, the batteries must be replaced approximately once a year to

Installing Smoke Detectors

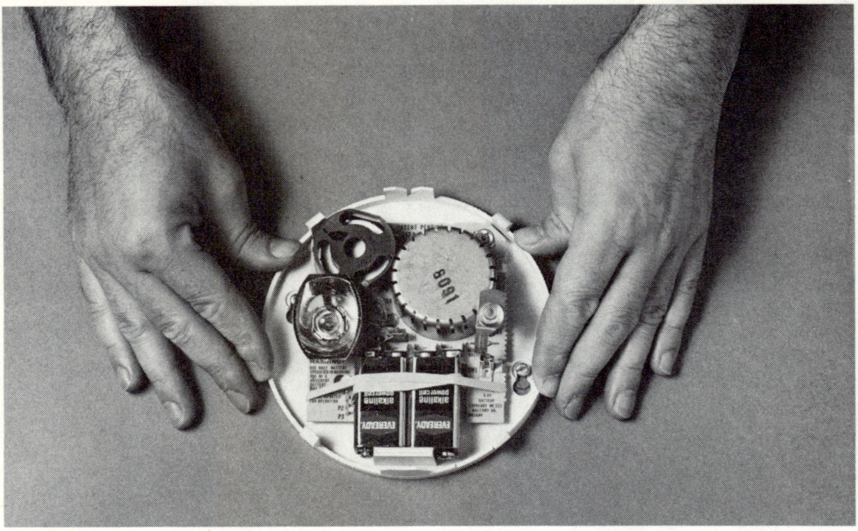

Remove cover by pulling away from base. Using base as a template, trace outline of the two keyhole slots.

This interconnectable detector is installed in the same way as any other battery or AC unit. To interconnect, pull leads from bottom of unit until knot in wire is firm against base. Run 22-gauge stranded wire to all detector locations. Attach stranded wire to interconnect leads with wire nuts, observing polarity, and mount detector base to ceiling or 4" junction box.

keep the detector operating properly. The cost of replacement batteries is between $2 and $10.

All UL-listed battery-operated smoke detectors are required to sound a trouble signal when the battery needs to be replaced. This "chirp" usually lasts seven days. If you are away from home for an extended period of time, it is advisable when you return to check your detector according to manufacturer's instructions, to make sure the battery has not lost power.

Smoke detectors that operate on household current can be powered in two ways. Equipped with an 8′ to 9′ electrical cord, they can be plugged into an existing wall outlet. A detector powered this way should not be operated with an on-off switch, because it may be accidentally turned off. It can also be wired permanently into your home's electrical system. This procedure requires an electrician, and the cost is usually between $25 and $50.

A fire in the home electrical circuit that would interrupt power to a smoke detector is a remote possibility. If an appliance, such as a TV set in the living room, starts the fire, a smoke detector located outside the bedroom area should sound an alarm before the fire reaches the electrical wiring. This is particularly true if the TV set and smoke detector are on different circuits.

Dirt, extreme changes in temperature, and cooking exhaust smoke can cause a false alarm or a malfunction in a smoke detector. To prevent false alarms, locate the detector away from air vents, air conditioners and fans. Keep the grillwork of the detector free of dirt by dusting or vacuuming it regularly. Check and replace batteries periodically. Test detectors every 30 days by using the test button, if provided, or by blowing smoke into the unit.

FIRE EXTINGUISHERS

■ Fire experts say that nearly all home fire fatalities could be prevented if fires were put out while small and isolated. This is the point at which the home fire extinguisher can be valuable. Prompt use of a portable extinguisher by a person who knows how to operate it can smother a small blaze before it spreads. If you are uncertain about the kind and size of fire extinguisher to buy, here are some basic facts.

Dry chemical extinguishers for home use have a cylindrical steel or aluminum shell filled with very fine, dry powdered chemicals and compressed nonflammable gas. Once the lever under the handle at

Even small grease fires can be potentially dangerous. You can protect your kitchen with a hand-operated portable fire extinguisher like this one.

the top of the cylinder is squeezed, the valve opens and the compressed gas forces the chemical through the nozzle in a fine spray. The range of the spray is from 5′ to 20′ and the extinguisher will empty itself in 10 to 25 seconds, depending on size and make.

Fire extinguishers have a gauge which tells you whether the cylinder is fully pressurized. Without full gas pressure, the dry chemical powder cannot be forced out of the cylinder and the extinguisher will not work. When buying an extinguisher always check the gauge to make sure the cylinder is fully pressurized.

Except for disposable types, most home fire extinguishers can be refilled with dry chemicals after they have been emptied. Refilling, pressurizing and resealing can be done only by the manufacturer's distributor, who has the special equipment for this purpose. Partially used extinguishers are no longer fully efficient and should be refilled and repressurized immediately.

Your owner's manual will give you complete instructions for operation, maintenance and recharging. The manufacturer's name and address will also be on the extinguisher nameplate.

EXTINGUISHER TYPES □ Fire extinguishers are marked with the letter A, B or C, according to the class of fire they fight.

Class A fires are fueled by wood, fabric, paper, rubber and most plastics.

Class B fires are fueled by flammable liquids such as oil, gasoline, paint or grease.

Class C fires are those in and around live electrical equipment such as appliances, radios and TV sets.

Two kinds of dry-chemical extinguishers are offered for home use. One is marked "Multipurpose A:B:C" and is effective against all three classes of fires. This type is filled with a dry chemical called monoammonium phosphate which interrupts the chemical chain reaction of the fire and, with ordinary combustibles, smothers the fire. The resultant residue acts as a fire retardant.

Multipurpose dry-chemical fire extinguishers come in various sizes according to the amount of agent they contain.

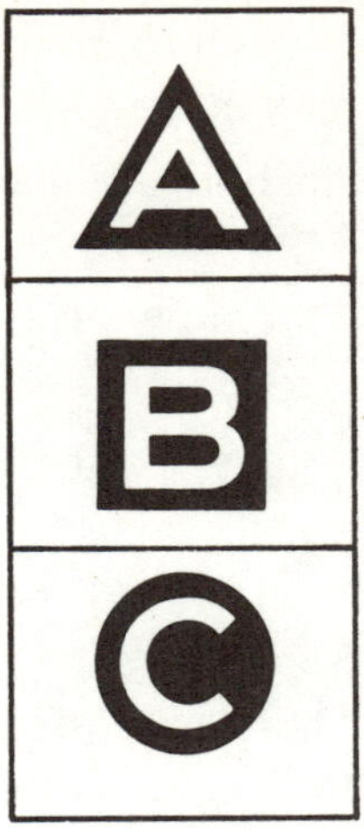

This symbol is found on water, multipurpose dry-chemical and foam extinguishers for use on ordinary combustibles such as wood, cloth, paper, rubber and most plastics.

This symbol is found on multipurpose dry-chemical, carbon dioxide and foam extinguishers for use on flammable or combustible liquids, flammable gases or similar materials.

This symbol is found on multipurpose dry-chemical and carbon dioxide extinguishers for use on fires involving energized electrical equipment.

Good locations for fire extinguishers include: corridor near door of bedroom, end wall cabinet next to kitchen door, hall near living room, tool rack near shop exit, and wall close to doors of garage and boat house.

The other type is filled with sodium bicarbonate (baking soda) and is used against Class B and C fires. The sodium bicarbonate interrupts the chemical process needed to keep the fire going by combining with grease to form a "soap" that is nonflammable and so can't be reignited.

Keep in mind that the sodium bicarbonate in B:C extinguishers does not work on burning wood, paper, fabric, etc. of Class A fires. Because house fires can be fueled from chemicals, wood, grease or other materials, a good all-around choice is the multipurpose A:B:C-rated extinguisher.

You can also find disposable foam-type extinguishers on the market. One is a small aerosol kitchen type which shoots a jet of foam. Rated 1B, it's disposable and effective against small grease or oil fires in frying pans and other utensils. Another disposable type has no pressure gauge, but has a button to indicate full pressure. It shoots dry chemicals at B:C fires.

UL LISTINGS □ UL stands for Underwriters Laboratories, a widely accepted independent, nonprofit organization that tests materials and products for hazards to life and property. All UL-tested fire equipment and nearly all extinguisher manufacturers are listed in the UL's Fire Protection Directory.

Two types of dry-chemical extinguishers are available for home use: multipurpose units effective against A, B and C fires; and sodium bicarbonate unit used against B and C fires.

Sodium bicarbonate fire extinguishers, like this American LaFrance unit, can be used on flammable liquids and electrical equipment.

Fire extinguishers are tested on actual fires that burn standard amounts or areas of wood or flammable liquids. The UL rating which appears on the label gives you a clear indication of the size and type of fire an extinguisher can cope with.

A rating of 1A-10 B:C means the extinguisher will put out a Class A fire of about 8 square feet and Class B and C fires of about 10 square feet. A rating of 2A, the most common for home extinguishers, covers about 10 square feet of Class A fire. B:C ratings correspond closely with square feet. Thus, 40 B:C means 40 square feet of coverage for those fires. The numbers are approximate—it isn't possible to measure a fire in exact square footage.

Home extinguishers may be 3″ to 7″ in diameter and weigh 16 to 20 pounds. The best size is the largest that the occupants of the house can handle easily and quickly. A typical 2A-10 B:C extinguisher containing 5 pounds of dry chemicals in a steel container may weigh 10 pounds. The same weight of dry chemicals in an aluminum container might have a weight of only $7^{1}/_{2}$ pounds. A realistic upper limit is 20 pounds gross weight. Don't be confused by the weight figure on the label.

FIRE ACTION PLAN

■ First of all, familiarize your family with the local fire department phone number. In more and more communities virtually all emer-

All-purpose fire extinguisher snuffs out engine fire. Extinguishers should be aimed at base of fire, not at flame or smoke.

gency services can be reached by dialing 911. Or apply adhesive stickers with fire and police emergency numbers on them to your phones. Or you can always dial "O." Decide which number you want your family to dial directly and have them practice with the receiver button down.

The best fire detection equipment can only tell you that there is a fire. All fire alarms should be used with a family escape plan. A smoke detector in working condition will usually give you at least three minutes to evacuate the house.

Just as schoolchildren practice fire drills to evacuate schools, your family should establish a plan and evacuation route. Rehearsed reaction to fire will help them stay calm and make an orderly retreat from a burning home.

The first rule for home fires, which often occur at night and in cold weather, is to get out. Take no possessions with you. Exit through prearranged paths, and assemble the family at a planned location so that everyone can be quickly accounted for.

Set up both a primary and secondary avenue of escape from a home fire. The primary route would likely be through halls to an outside exit. The secondary route would probably be through a window. Because smoke and fumes spread rapidly through the house, it's advantageous for everyone in the family to sleep with bedroom doors closed. This also prevents drafts, which cause fires to spread more rapidly.

In the event fire is detected, drop to hands and knees, and crawl to the bedroom door. Place your hand against the door; if the door is not hot to the touch, open it and proceed through halls and outside. If the door is hot, use your secondary exit through a window. Make sure all windows can be easily opened so a child can get out. If the window cannot be opened, use a chair or other furniture to break the glass.

Do not permit your family to sleep in areas where there is no secondary escape route. This applies particularly to basement areas where small windows high on the wall prevent a person from getting out.

If clothing catches on fire, do not run. Running fans the flames, and severe burns may result. Drop to the floor or ground and roll over, smothering the flames. If you see a person with clothing aflame, wrap a coat or blanket around them and roll them on the ground.

Use a location well away from the house as an assembly point. When all members of the family are accounted for, go to the nearest phone and call the fire department.

ESCAPE EQUIPMENT

■ Second- and third-story leaps for life are great for high school athletes and for dramatic front page news photos. But infants, the elderly and the handicapped as well as people trapped in an upper-story room require special help if they're to get out of a fire alive.

Three types of devices help facilitate the upper-story exit: the metal escape ladder (folding or permanently installed); the rope ladder (plain, knotted or even fabricated from chain); and the fireman's pole.

You have several choices in ladders. Commercially available equipment includes concealable types that fasten to a permanently installed eyebolt under the window. Another type of permanent installation is the folding ladder which mounts on the wall below a window. It is stored in the closed position, then opened from the window when needed. To benefit from this device, you need to install one below each bedroom. The disadvantage to any permanent ladder installation is that the room with the ladder might be blocked off by the spreading fire.

Portable chain-type ladders provide some flexibility, but they still may not be accessible to all family members. Also, getting a commercial rope-type ladder to hang properly can be tricky.

You can show your family how to knot a sheet; be sure to stress that the knotted sheet or rope must be tied to a radiator or heavy bedstead and checked quickly before trusting any weight to it. Having this skill can ensure escape no matter what other equipment is available.

A fireman's pole is easy and inexpensive to install. You may want to place two or three at critical points around the house. After you have located the upper-story exit points, estimate the distance the smallest member of the family can reach out from the window (12″ to 18″ if you have young children). Locate the position for the top fitting first, then use a plumb-bob to find the dead-center location for the lower sleeve. Next, plot the dimensions of the concrete footing at the base. Once both upper and lower fittings are in place, insert a 1½″- to 2″-diameter pole into the upper fixture until it clears the bottom sleeve, swing it over the sleeve and let it drop into place.

Valuable papers can be kept secure from fire if stored in a fire-rated safe. A variety of styles and sizes are available; some can be used as furniture. This modestly priced unit (left) saved its contents for one hour in a 1,700°F fire (right).

VALUABLE PAPERS

■ Many homeowners feel that home safes are only to protect expensive jewels, heirlooms or other valuables from burglars. The truth is that most burglars who can lift a safe will carry it away and open it at their leisure. The main reason for buying an economically priced fire-rated home safe is to protect valuable papers every homeowner has which would be difficult to replace.

The following list of items should be considered for safekeeping in case of fire:

——fire insurance policy
——birth certificate
——mortgage
——stocks and bonds
——theft insurance policy
——bank statements
——life, health or other insurance policies
——stamp collection
——coin collection
——family photographs
——wills
——tax records and returns
——receipts for valuables
——jewelry
——marriage certificate
——manuscripts
——discharge papers
——college degrees
——Social Security card
——documented photographs
——copy of driver's license and car registration
——educational transcripts
——title to cemetery lot
——jewelry appraisals
——home business records
——extra checks and deposit records
——keys for safe-deposit box
——loan agreements
——working or immigration papers
——medical records
——deeds
——family death certificate
——apartment or office lease
——garage lease
——contracts and other legal documents
——letters
——family tree or crest
——cash
——business records
——adoption papers
——Veteran's Administration claim
——trust instruments
——passport photos
——credit card numbers
——safe number
——others

Do-It-Yourself Disaster-Proofing

CHAPTER 11 ■ At any given moment, there are 1,800 storms in progress on the face of the earth. Lightning strikes 100 times a second. In one year, ocean-born cyclones hurl an average of a half-dozen hurricanes against U.S. coasts, killing between 50 and 100 people and leaving $100 million or more in property damage and injuries. Tornadoes sweep across the Great Plains taking another dozen or so lives yearly, causing untold destruction to buildings, livestock and crops.

Natural disasters may be predicted (see Chapter 9 for information on storm detectors). But they are events that you can do little to avoid. As with fire, the key to survival and comfort is advance preparation. There are a number of measures you as a homeowner can take to prepare yourself for such potential disasters as floods, hurricanes, cyclones, tornadoes, severe winds and blizzards.

BLACKOUT PROTECTION

■ Blackouts caused by interruption of electrical power due to storms and other technical failures are occurring more and more often. Today you can take the sting out of power failures by buying and installing portable power plants to keep freezers, refrigerators, heating systems and some lights going. Portable power plants provide instant electricity with the pull of a rope or the push of a button.

Manufacturers offer a wide assortment of units that use gasoline engines to supply 120v and/or 240v alternating current. Both generators and alternators are available. A generator uses a stationary magnetic field and revolving coils of wire (armature); an alternator uses a revolving magnetic field rotar within stationary coils of wire (stator).

Smaller units are handy for powering a host of shop and garden tools in the backyard or "back 40," as well as other power-users like TV sets, radios and hair dryers. But units that supply 3,000 watts or more can be readily adapted to provide standby power for your home during a blackout or temporary power interruption. Although 3,000 watts is much less than the power your home normally requires, it's enough to provide essential energy until utility power is restored.

To be ready for utility power failure, plan to have the required transfer and connection devices installed when you buy your portable power plant. Electrical codes require that a licensed electrician make the connections. Here's how it's done.

A weatherproof connection box is installed outside your home, generally near the utility company meter. A transfer switch is installed beside the primary home-load center (circuit-breaker box or fuse box). The main utility company line is connected to the transfer

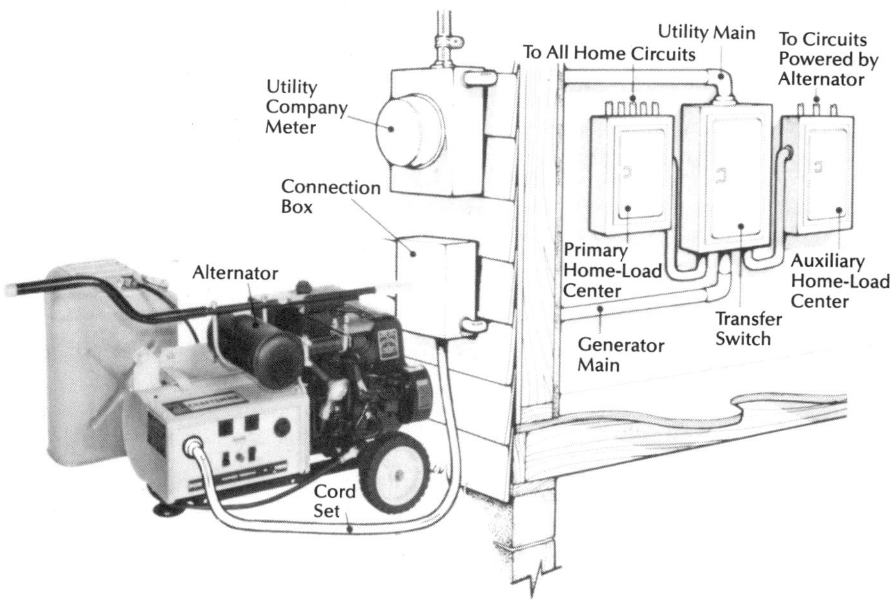

How one portable power plant hooks up for home power station. The best bet is to leave installation to a licensed pro.

switch, and a new primary feed run back from the transfer switch to the home-load center.

Another feed line goes to an auxiliary home-load center. This is another circuit-breaker box, with its output wiring connected only to essential circuits that are to be fed by the power plant. The power plant main is joined to the transfer switch by the connection box. When the utility company is feeding power, the transfer switch routes it to the primary home-load center for distribution to all circuits in the household.

When utility power fails, you connect the portable power plant to the outside connection box, and the engine is started. Flipping the transfer switch to its opposite position now connects power from your auxiliary unit to the essential circuits of your home. This fool-proof system gives you a complete, safe and convenient way to ride out a power failure.

Note: All circuits of your home are completely disconnected from the utility company main by the transfer switch, so there will be no problem when utility power comes back on.

BUYING A UNIT □ Portable power plants are compact members of a larger family of gas-driven power plants. Relatively light, the smallest weigh about 60 pounds. Powered by engines rated from 3 to 16 hp, output ranges from 1,500 watts for the smallest to 7,000 watts for the huskiest models.

Some newer units are specially designed for home installations. Others are compact enough to take with you in the trunk of a full-size car, to stow in a camper, or to keep handy in the garage or toolshed for occasional or backup power. Many models are available on wheeled carts to ease maneuvering. The units furnish alternating current like that available from your household power outlets. The speed of the engine is governed so that the frequency (rate at which the current reverses) is closely held to 60 Hz (or times per second). The power output is the product of its voltage and current. At 120 volts with a maximum current of 12½ amperes, a unit has an output rating of 1,500 watts.

Power output depends on the engine doing the work. The formula used is 746 watts = 1 hp. That means to get 1,500 watts, the engine must furnish at least 2 hp. In use, an engine will be rated at somewhat greater horsepower to account for normal losses in the conversion of mechanical energy (hp) into electrical energy (watts). Typical efficiencies of units range from 60% to 70%.

Power plants come in various configurations and sizes. Pincor 4,500-watt unit (left) mounts on lawn or garden tractor. Others (clockwise from top right) include Generac's 3,750-watt extended-run model; McCulloch's Mite-E-Lite unit in a 3,300-watt version with cradle frame; Generac's enclosed, fully automatic 5,000-watt model; Ag-Tronic's generator, available in 4,500- and 6,000-watt models.

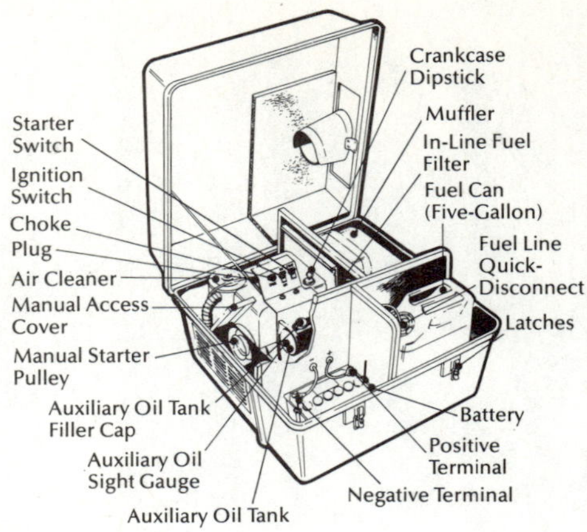

New standby power plant from Homelite, built specifically to protect homes in emergencies, is self-contained. The 210-pound unit delivers a 5,000-watt output to run your heating system, refrigerator and a limited number of lights and appliances. To use, you lift cover of ABS all-weather enclosure, push start and ignition buttons, flip 30-amp circuit breaker to "on," then throw transfer switch.

FEATURES TO CHECK □ Power output is the real key to buying the right power plant. Determine your maximum power need by adding up the wattages used by various electrical devices. If more than one device will be powered at a time, add their wattages. Next add a safety factor of 20% to account for variations in load from devices during start-up. Most models have a surge capacity rating to allow for this start-up.

Buy the unit that has the nearest higher wattage rating. That is, if you add up a need for 1,600 watts, don't try to get by with a 1,500-watt unit. You'll shorten its life span because the normal load exceeds the unit's capacity. Rather, buy one rated at 2,000 watts. It will run more smoothly for a longer time because it has reserve capacity. Other features to check include the following:

Noise level □ The engine in some cases will be running outdoors for prolonged periods. Choose a unit with an effective muffler system that reduces engine noise to the lowest practical level. Consider where and when you will be using the unit. If it will be running in a location that's within earshot of you or your neighbors, get the quietest design you can find.

Fuel capacity □ Too small a fuel capacity means annoying stop-and-go refueling periods. Your unit should run for at least 90 minutes at rated power output on a single fueling. Some manufacturers offer additional long-run features—a gas and oil reserve supply that allows a six- to 24-hour refueling interval.

Interference □ You may wish to power radio, TV or communications equipment. If so, be sure that the ignition system of the unit's engine has the latest interference-suppression controls.

Outlets and extras □ To simplify connecting the power unit to the device it will power, built-in AC outlets are provided. Some units

Larger portables are able to supply enough electricity to keep your home going through a power failure. Note outlets, overload switch and built-in low-voltage DC charging terminals.

provide more than one outlet, and some offer both 120v and 240v output. But remember that the total power delivered to all devices plugged into these outlets must not exceed the unit's output rating. Some, such as those from Sears, have built-in overload warning lights, and feature spark-arrest mufflers.

For short-circuit protection, look for fuses or a circuit breaker in the unit. Also, if you need to charge batteries from time to time, you may want to consider a unit that provides 12v DC output. Some units can provide up to 10 amps of charging power for batteries in outdoor equipment, recreational vehicles and remote-control equipment.

If your portable power plant includes a battery-recharge feature, the general hookup procedure is as follows: Connect the positive terminal of the battery to the positive terminal of the generator. Then connect the negative terminal of the battery to the positive terminal of the alternator. Start the engine. The battery will receive an initial high charge of several amperes, reducing to a trickle as the battery comes up to strength.

USING A POWER PLANT □ Set the unit up on a fairly level surface in the open. When starting, it's best to disconnect the unit from any load. Once the engine has come up to speed and is providing full output, you can plug in the load. If current drain is substantial you may notice a variation in the engine sound at start-up as the unit commences to supply power to the load. This will smooth out as current flow stabilizes.

Most portables include a quick-stop feature to permit rapid shutoff should trouble occur. The preferred method of stopping is to unplug the load and allow the engine to run for a few minutes to reduce its operating temperature before shutoff. Following are tips to help you operate a unit safely:

- Never operate the unit in an enclosed space. Provide adequate ventilation as a safeguard against deadly carbon monoxide. The unit also generates heat, and if run in an enclosed area the heat might melt the plastic gas tank.

- Never fill the gas tank while the engine is running or in the dark. Gas spillage on a hot engine can cause fire or explosion. Store gas properly.

- Power units produce lethal voltages, and should be treated with respect. Maintain power cords in good condition—bare or frayed wires can cause dangerous electrical shock. Be sure the unit is properly grounded according to manufacturer's instructions.

▪ Check engine oil level each time you fill the gas tank. Study the owner's manual carefully before operating your unit.

▪ Never attempt to change engine speed without proper knowledge and equipment. Incorrect engine rpm can damage the alternator or the equipment it powers.

EMERGENCY LIGHTING □ Even if you have an emergency power plant to take over during electrical interruptions, you may want to have alternate lighting available. Besides candles, flashlights and gas or kerosene lanterns, you can buy newer security lights which plug into an electrical outlet and provide light during emergencies. The unit shown in the photo may also be used as a portable flashlight or as a night-light for a kitchen, bathroom or child's room.

This security light provides illumination during emergencies such as those caused by power failures. It costs less than $15.

This security light draws its power from household current; when plugged in, it is charged when the switch is set at "auto." Its three-position switch has "on" for use as a flashlight, "auto" for use as a power failure light and for recharging, and "off" for recharging only.

LIGHTNING-PROOFING

■ At least 18,000 homes and 12,000 other buildings in the U.S. are destroyed or damaged annually by lightning.

Lightning is electricity with extremely high voltage (pressure) and amperage (rate of electrical flow). Ordinary house current has from 110 to 240 volts and about 100 amperes. This current can be lethal and, if shorted, cause fires. Most lightning fires, damage and casualties are caused by direct strikes to the roof, chimney or dormer of the house. Antennas and trees are often struck, and bolts then jump to plumbing or wiring. Trees shattered by lightning can send limbs weighing several hundred pounds smashing down on a home.

BUILDING PROTECTION □ Statistics on home and farm fires show lightning is consistently to blame for about 50% of insurance loss claims. Unprotected wood-sided houses with ordinary roofing are easily set on fire by lightning. Masonry, concrete and frame walls are susceptible to the explosive effects of a lightning bolt.

Buildings can be protected against damage by installing one of the following devices suggested by Underwriters Laboratories:

■ Lightning rods. Connected by cable to grounding equipment, they serve as a path by which lightning can travel harmlessly into the ground.

■ Secondary service arresters. Connected from incoming electrical wiring and distribution circuits to grounding equipment, they safely divert any high voltage surge in wiring caused by a bolt in the vicinity of power lines.

■ Antenna lightning discharge units. These protect TVs, radios and CB receivers hooked up to outdoor antennas from damage by surges in voltage, and are connected between an outdoor antenna and the ground.

What do you need? The illustration shows your options. City homes are often better protected than those in the country by inter-

Lightning protection points of a house include: 1) terminals spaced a minimum of 20′ apart along ridges and within 2′ of ridge ends; 2) down-lead conductors; 3) a minimum of two grounds at least 10′ deep for house, and additional grounds for clotheslines, etc.; 4) roof ornaments tied into conductor system; 5) protection for any tree within 10′ of house connected to house grounding; 6) at least two terminals on chimneys; 7) rods for dormers; 8) arrester on antenna connected to main conductor; 9) tie-in to conductor system or gutter within 6′ of conductor; 10) arrester on overhead power lines.

ception from taller buildings, streetlights and poles carrying electrical power.

TREE PROTECTION □ You can't prevent lightning from striking trees near your home, but by installing a lightning protection system for trees you can make them safe from damage and keep them from causing damage. The idea is to ground the bolt harmlessly so it doesn't go through the wood. A proper tree protection system has:

1. A main air terminal, placed as high as possible in the tree's branches.
2. Strategically placed smaller air terminals on main branches.
3. A 17-gauge conductor to connect the air terminals to the ground.
4. Two copper or copper-clad ground rods, buried 10′ in the ground.

The system is inconspicuous and does not damage the tree. It's

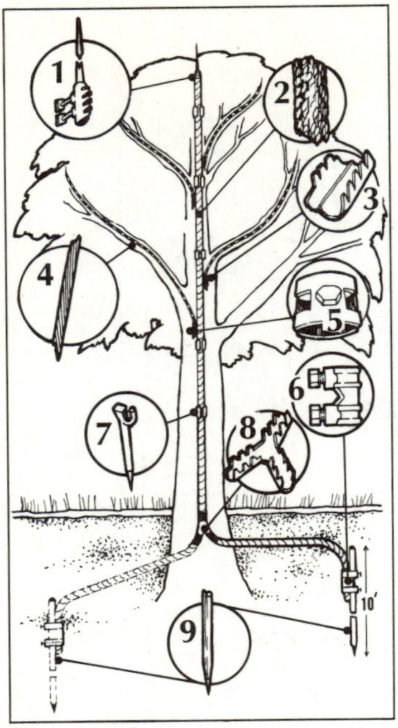

Detailed here are the essential components of a lightning protection system for a tree: 1) special tree point or terminal; 2) standard tree conductor; 3) finger-type conductor; 4) typical branch connections; 5) conductor clamp; 6) ground rod clamp; 7) conductors leading from branches and conductor fastener; 8) forked ground connector; and 9) ground rod.

designed so the conductor cables unloop and "grow" with the tree.

A Lightning Protection Institute study shows that oak, elm and pine trees are most often struck by lightning. However, other species are also likely targets, because the location or prominence of a tree is what makes it vulnerable. If the tree in your yard is taller than your house, or if it is a lone tree or the tallest in a grove, the odds are good that it will be hit by lightning.

As part of a complete lightning protection system, a properly grounded tree will help protect not only the house, but people as well. During storms, people trapped outdoors often take shelter under a tree. Proper grounding reduces the likelihood that someone under the tree will be hurt. Fencing a tree to keep people 6′ away from the trunk reduces the danger of injury from a side flash of lightning from the tree.

INSIDE PROTECTION □ You can protect your home from the inside as well, using lightning protection devices installed on your home's circuit-breaker load center. Lightning striking near power lines can result in surges of thousands of volts which travel down the power lines seeking a circuit path to the ground. If the surge enters your home, extensive damage to appliances and wiring can occur.

One appliance protector made by General Electric dissipates an excessive voltage surge within a fraction of a second after it enters the house to prevent damage to refrigerators, washers, dryers, pumps, furnaces and other electrical equipment. The device is best installed by a qualified electrician—it's possible, when attempting to install these units, to come in contact with dangerous voltages or to incorrectly install the unit and render it ineffective.

For even more protection for solid state equipment like stereos and televisions, General Electric recommends that a lightning protector be used in conjunction with another device available called a voltage spike protector. An electrician can explain what you need for total protection.

PERSONAL PROTECTION □ You can also take steps to ensure your personal safety from lightning. Outdoors, take cover in a building, ditch or ravine. Avoid golf courses, fences, trees, telephone poles, exposed sheds and power lines. Stay out of water and open boats. In a car, avoid power lines or trees which could fall. Otherwise, cars usually offer good protection.

Indoors, avoid metal objects, plumbing, sinks and tubs, radiators

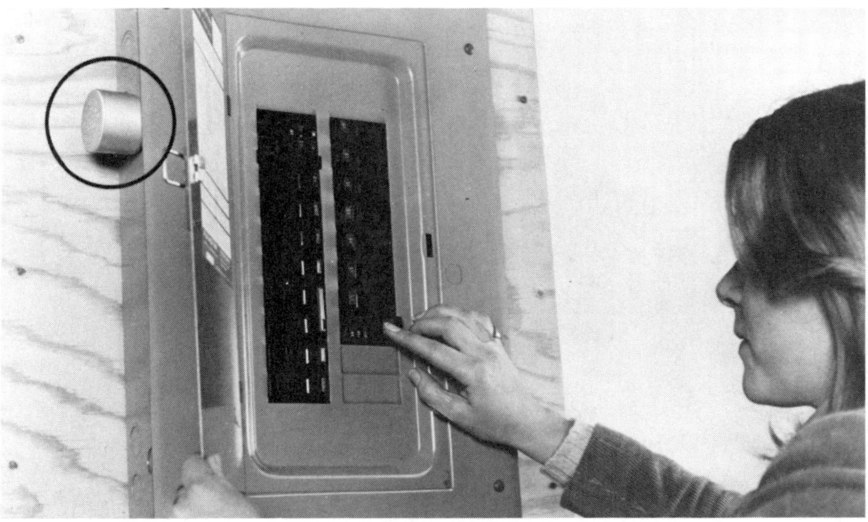

Installed on the circuit-breaker load center (circled), lightning protection device dissipates excessive voltage surges which can damage appliances and possibly cause fire.

Mean monthly number of tornadoes by state.

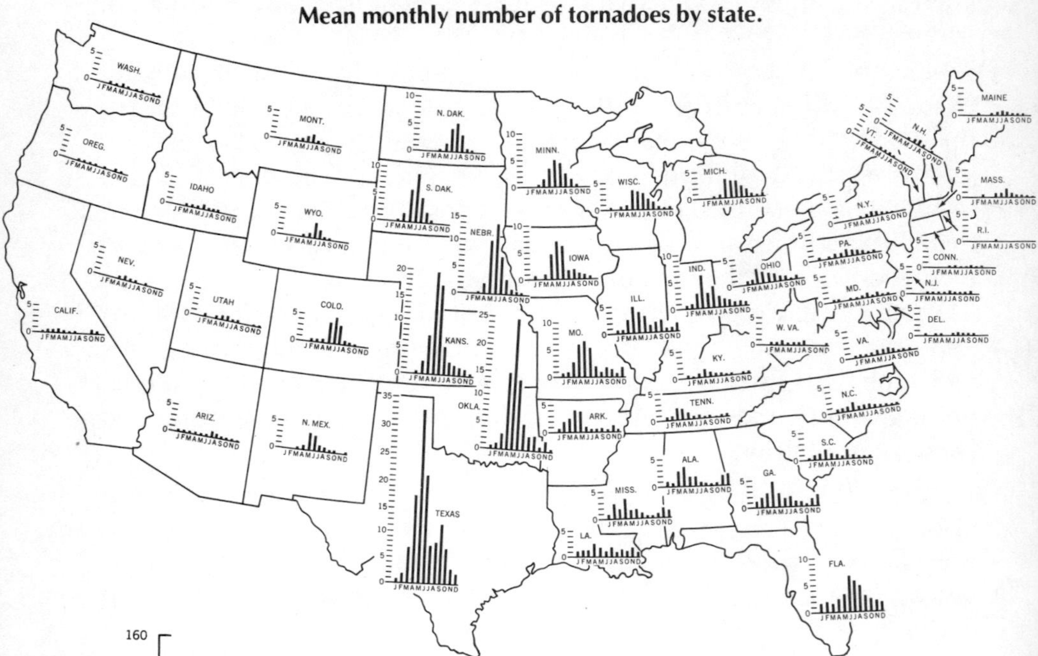

BASED ON PERIOD 1953-76

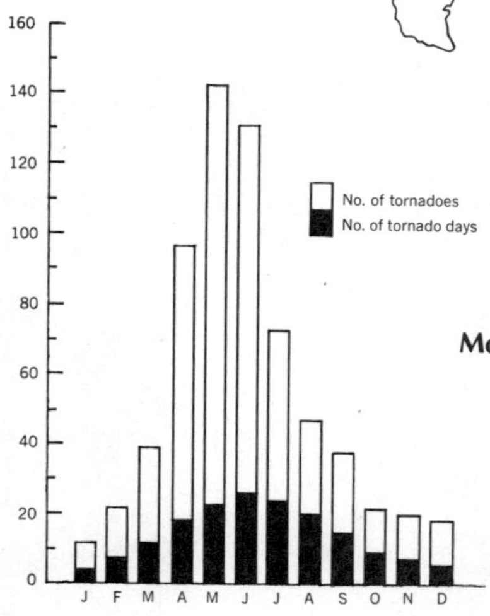

Monthly number of tornado days in U.S.

Average monthly number of tornado days in the United States, 1953-71 (12,444 tornadoes reported.)

and stoves. Stay away from fireplaces, open doors and windows, and porches. Do not use telephones or appliances.

STORM PROTECTION

■ Storms and floods pose the biggest threat to homeowners in this country. Some major earthquakes have taken their toll in life and property, but year in and year out, it's hurricanes, tornadoes, severe winds and floods that are of the greatest concern to homeowners.

Though you don't hear much about bomb shelters anymore, several types of well-stocked home shelters originally designed for protection from fallout offer safety from natural disasters as well. Some of these shelters can be do-it-yourself projects costing about $150, while more complex shelters require considerably more money, plus the help of a competent building contractor.

Plans for construction of home shelters are available through your local civil defense director or your local agricultural extension service. Building-supply dealers and contractors can also give you advice and plans for home shelters. Local authorities can tell you how to stock your home shelter so your family can be self-sustaining during emergencies.

Following are last-minute steps to prepare yourself and family for potential disasters:

- Keep listening to the radio for latest local information. Have a battery-powered radio in case of electrical failure, complete with batteries.
- Gather food supplies that don't need cooking or refrigeration, and store them in or near your shelter. Also collect additional items you may need, including eating and cooking utensils, can opener, storm and first-aid manuals, first-aid supplies, special medicines, bedding, clothing, a large covered container for human waste disposal, flash-

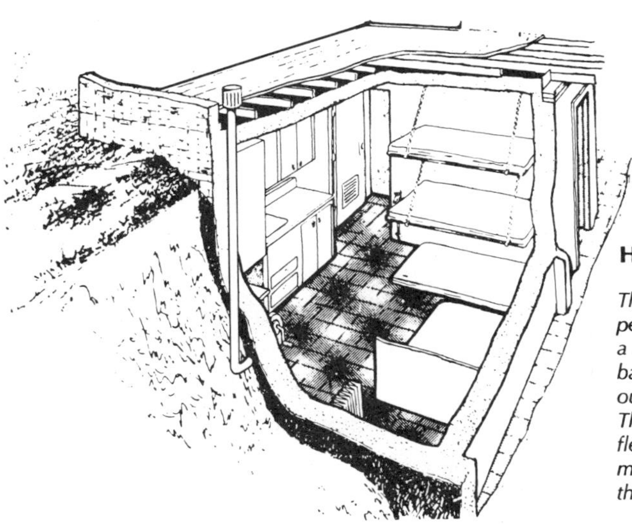

Home Shelters

This basement shelter for six persons is intended to be built with a new house, in a corner of the basement where earth on the outside wall reaches the ceiling. The shelter has multiple uses and flexible shape, and utilizes materials and labor that tie in with the home's construction.

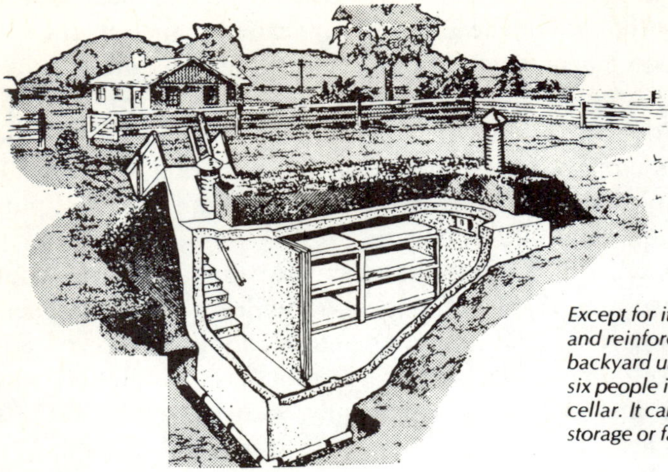

Except for its heavier construction and reinforced entrance, this backyard underground shelter for six people is similar to a cyclone cellar. It can be used as a storm, storage or fallout shelter.

This basement sand-filled lumber lean-to protects three people. The home itself gives partial protection, while the sandbags block the ends of the shelter. It's low in cost and simple to build.

lights and extra batteries, candles, matches, lanterns, newspapers, plastic and paper bags, paper towels, disinfectant, toilet articles and religious materials.

■ Fill all available clean containers with fresh water. If possible, have about seven gallons of water for each person. Be prepared to disinfect water during emergencies by boiling it for three minutes or adding 16 drops of liquid chlorine laundry bleach or tincture of iodine to each gallon of water.

■ When storms are approaching, find the safest place for those at home before you send anyone after absent family members. Use your shelter, storm cellar, basement corner or whatever area you've planned to use in emergencies. For windstorms or fallout, turn off the gas supply to all appliances except the furnace. Turn off the main water valve if there is no pressure.

TORNADOES □ In case of a threatening tornado go to the basement if you have no special shelter. The best corner of your basement runs from the junction of the two walls furthest underground, about 10′ along each side. This is the place to take shelter during a tornado if you're unsure about where the storm may come from. Otherwise go to the corner the funnel is expected to strike last. If you have no basement, crawl under heavy furniture in the center of your house. Stay in your shelter until you are certain the danger has passed.

Leave windows open on the side of the house away from the tornado. This helps equalize the air pressure inside your house.

FLOODS □ For floods, evacuate immediately when you are advised to do so. Take necessities such as medications, eye glasses, diet foods and suitable clothing with you. If you have time, collect valuables and legal papers, and move items such as food, furniture, rugs, appliances, clothing, books, electric motors and controls to higher elevations.

Whether you need to evacuate your home or not, observe these precautions:

- Shut off all utilities at main switches and valves.
- Fill all portions of your home's water system with clean water and cap all openings.
- Seal wells to keep out silt and debris.
- Allow indoor and outdoor water levels to equalize by leaving doors and windows open. This will help prevent foundations from collapsing and buildings from floating away.
- Keep out mud and silt by flooding the basement with clean water.

WINTER STORMS □ To prepare for winter storms, maintain an ample supply of heating fuel, at least sufficient to last beyond a three-day storm. If possible, have another way to keep your family warm in case of extended electrical failure. Plan to use your fireplace, space heater and/or emergency setup for your gas furnace, and have a supply of warm bedding and clothing on hand. Also plan for emergency lighting equipment if you don't have a power generator, plus emergency cooking facilities. Stay indoors.

AFTER A DISASTER

■ The aftermath of a natural disaster can persist for weeks. This puts an incredible burden on authorities, since it is largely their role to stimulate and direct the recovery effort.

Your participation in recovery could be particularly valuable if you have special skills or expertise that others lack. But even if all you can lend to the effort is a strong back and rudimentary first-aid ability, your help will be appreciated by your community. Just keeping your family calmly together until rescue workers arrive will contribute to the recovery effort.

Consider taking a first-aid course soon. If you've had first-aid training, now is a good time to update it.

In the aftermath of a major storm you may be able to help others get first aid, food and shelter; take steps to prevent or control fires; report locations of loose power lines and broken sewer, water and gas mains to officials; assist in rescue operations, relief work or the recovery and identification of the dead; ration food supplies reduced by spoilage or contamination; and stay away from areas of more serious destruction unless specifically requested to help.

AFTER A FLOOD □ You can help by making sure everyone is safe from new flood crests, fires and collapsing buildings. You can help arrange for shelter, food, clothing, transportation and medical care for those in need. Cooperate as best you can with local authorities.

Test your plumbing by flushing it out with buckets of water. Have your sanitary disposal system and water supply tested by health authorities. Boil or chlorinate water for emergency drinking. Destroy all food that has been in contact with flood water.

Clean and dry your home out before moving back in. Use flashlights, not matches, when you first enter the building. Don't use the electrical system until it has been tested by an electrician. Also wait until surrounding flood waters are below basement floor level before pumping or draining the basement. The additional pressure of saturated ground may cause basement walls to collapse.

If possible, use stoves and heating systems to help with the drying-out process. Remove sediment from heaters and flues, and be sure electric motors are dry before using them. Dry and air clothing, bedding, furniture and rugs as soon as possible to prevent mildew. Try to control rodents and insects. Delay permanent repairs until the home is thoroughly dry.

Electronic Alarm Systems

CHAPTER 12 ■ Of all the things social scientists, police and criminologists have learned through years of research and investigation into crime, the most basic is that the threat of immediate discovery is the most powerful deterrent. Nothing increases the threat of discovery to a burglar like the racket raised by a good, loud alarm system, morning, noon or night. Effective systems range in price from $75 to over $2,000. It's simply a matter of understanding your own needs and accordingly tailoring the equipment you buy.

First, some basics. Electronic security systems are available in three basic versions—hardwired, line-carrier and wireless. The hardwired systems use their own wires. Line-carrier systems use the electrical circuitry in your home to carry signals. Wireless units use infrared light, microwaves, radio frequencies or ultrasonic sound waves. Consider using either wired or wireless systems. Good hardwired systems have self-supervised circuits, and even if a wire is cut alarms will sound. Both hardwired and wireless systems should have standby battery power.

PARTS OF AN ALARM SYSTEM

■ All security alarms are made up of three basic parts—sensors, a control unit and the actual alarm. While some systems are self-contained and house all three components in one unit, you'll find the most flexibility in systems where each part is separate.

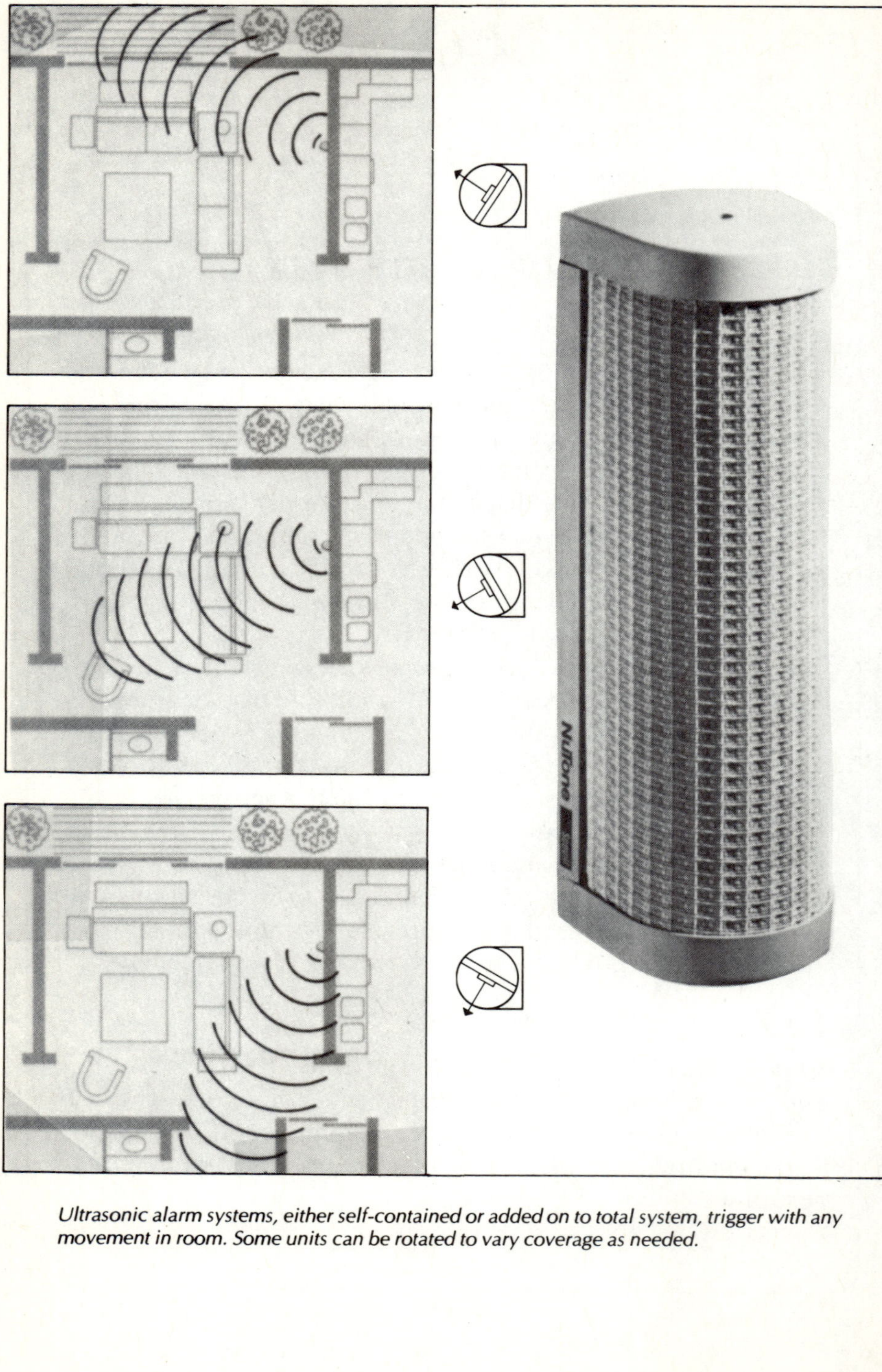

Ultrasonic alarm systems, either self-contained or added on to total system, trigger with any movement in room. Some units can be rotated to vary coverage as needed.

HOW SENSORS WORK □ The sensor's function is to detect an intrusion. Once the sensor has been disturbed, it sends a signal to the control unit, which in turn triggers the alarm. Panic or emergency buttons can also be connected to the control unit so you can actuate the alarm manually. The alarm functions to attract attention to the fact that a break-in is occurring. This can be done with a local alarm—a bell or siren you or your neighbors can hear—or with a prerecorded telephone message sent to a monitoring station.

Sensors and panic buttons can be connected to the control unit either by direct wiring or by a wireless system. The wireless system operates on batteries that must be changed periodically. Transmitters are installed at each sensor or panic button and a receiver is installed in the control unit. The wireless panic button can be carried from room to room.

The following are some of the more commonly available sensors or detectors:

Switch sensors □ These electromagnetic devices can be installed at all entry points accessible from the ground. When a door or window is opened, the alarm is triggered. It is advisable to install sensors on windows or balcony doors adjacent to trees. Switch sensors are the most popular alarm sensors for homes.

Pressure mats □ These devices protect specific areas of the home. They can be hidden under a carpet or rug in a frequently traveled corridor or can be used near items of value such as a TV set or stereo system. When pressure is exerted on the mat, the alarm is triggered.

Ultrasonic motion detectors □ These fill the room with sound waves too high for most humans to hear. Any movement in the room disturbs the wave pattern and triggers the alarm. Inexpensive ultrasonic motion detectors operating at 20 Hz can be heard by humans and dogs; more expensive units operating at 40 Hz cannot be heard. Because some people and most animals are bothered by high-pitched sounds, an in-home demonstration before purchasing is advisable.

Infrared photoelectric sensors □ With these, an infrared light beam is projected between two points. Anything interrupting the beam will trigger an alarm. They are effective when installed at entry points as well as specific areas inside your home.

TYPES OF ALARMS □ There are two types of reporting alarms available—local and remote.

The local alarm is the simplest to install and the least expensive. When the system detects an intruder the alarm signal is heard at or near your home. Its effectiveness depends on the intruder being frightened away or neighbors calling the police. The alarm device is generally located in the attic or under the eaves of the roof.

The remote alarm transmits the alarm signal to a location away from your home, but can be combined with a local alarm. Several types of remote alarms are available, including:

Automatic dialer □ This alarm sends a prerecorded message or signal over telephone lines to an answering service, a neighbor or a relative. The effectiveness of this system depends on someone being present to answer the telephone and call the police. The telephone company requires that the installation of a dialer system meet its specifications.

Note: Do not direct your alarm to the local police department without prior approval. Several of the first dialer alarms were so unreliable that many jurisdictions prohibit directing an alarm from a dialer to a police department.

Direct-connect system □ Here, the alarm signal is transmitted to the police department. This type of service provides very good protection, but often is not available to the private homeowner. Most jurisdictions limit the direct-connect service to financial institutions and commercial establishments. The signals are carried over leased lines and there is a monthly charge to the subscriber.

Central-station system □ This commercial service transmits the alarm signal to a private security company that monitors the system. In addition to notifying the police that your system has sent an alarm, the central station will dispatch guards to your home. Central stations will normally include the maintenance and repair of your alarm system as a part of your contract and will charge a monthly service fee.

THE COMPREHENSIVE ALARM SYSTEM

■The first question to answer is whether you want to design and install an alarm system yourself by using components off the shelf, buy a prepackaged system, or deal with an established alarm company such as Honeywell, Westinghouse, ADT or Rollins.

The success you have in boosting your home's security can be directly affected by the type of alarm system you select. A loud on-the-spot alarm may chase most burglars away. Some burglars put up with such alarms and depend on their speed and knowledge of the area to make a getaway before police arrive. Burglars who enter a house with an alarm that is silent in the home but rings at a central station may not be aware that the alarm has been set off, so take their time and end up being arrested at the scene of the crime.

Any alarm system of modest sophistication can run up to several hundred dollars; very little in the way of alarm company services are available for less than $1,000. But the service companies do offer advantages that may outweigh price: central office alarm-system monitoring, the guarantee of someone available to call the police and meet them at your door if the alarm goes off, full maintenance and service backup, extensive expertise to assist you in designing the system, and carrying out a high-grade installation. In addition, they can help you realize higher discounts on your homeowners insurance premiums.

As a do-it-yourselfer, you might be able to conceal wiring and sensor systems, give a control box a built-in look and minimize the system's exposure to would-be burglars and vandals. But there is no doubt that the alarm companies have the edge in technical expertise, testing, tools and pure experience.

Another consideration is your electronic orientation. Market researchers estimate that because few people other than experienced do-it-yourselfers have a good grasp of electronic principles, nine out of ten purchasers will have their alarm system installed. But the fact is that you don't have to be an Edison to handle this type of project —the barriers are mostly psychological. And if you're a little fuzzy on terms like "electromagnet," "relay" and "ultrasonics," bone up on electricity basics right in the beginning.

Whether you handle the installation of your system yourself or hire a service to do it for you, the principles of planning a system are the same. The better you understand what you can and cannot accomplish with a home-security system, the better use you'll make of your security dollar.

PLANNING YOUR SYSTEM □ Your first and most crucial step is to identify problem areas in and around your house. The one way *not* to approach this is to try to "play burglar." Second-guessing a

14-year-old youth who may be under the influence of thrill-seeking peers, alcohol, other drugs or his own sense of adventure is certain to lead nowhere.

Stick to the evidence at hand. Remember that many successful residential burglaries involve the opening of an outside door—if not for entry, almost certainly to provide an escape route. If all you do is bug the ground-level doors and balcony doors where a natural climbing route exists, you will sharply reduce the chances of loss due to burglary. Remember too that once the alarm goes off, only a stone-deaf thief is going to persist with his shenanigans or fumble his way to an alternate entry point.

A sensible system will involve adequate protection of all openings large enough for a person to enter, at or below the height of 12′. Each of these openings is a prime candidate for a sensor, or bug.

This approach emphasizes only the exterior, or what people in the alarm business call the "perimeter" of the area to be protected. Some inside portions of your home are also logical locations for sensors, especially those that cover zones rather than just points of entry. Such sensors may detect sound, pressure or movement.

If you have several windows and a door all providing access to a common hall or a room containing no valuables, you might consider installing a sensor in the passageway from that room to the rest of the house. Sensors designed for zone coverage are harder to spot and therefore harder to evade or defeat than electromechanical sensors located where the burglar has learned to look for them—windows, doorways, outer landings and the like.

The best approach is to combine perimeter with interior protection. By installing both motion-detecting sensors and the simpler electromechanical bugs, you can trip up the burglar after he penetrates your outer defenses and starts moving toward your valuables.

Don't forget to make some provisions for the master bedroom. Figures show it to be the most frequently violated interior space of the home. Coverage of the hall leading to the master bedroom, a sensor on the door, or window switches alone or in combination with one another can be used effectively.

One caution: Design a system you and your family can live with. Multiplying sensors and loading up on ultrasonics and microwave units can sometimes create more nuisance than protection. Remember that a system that constantly puts out false alarms will neither endear you to your neighbors nor encourage a prompt response

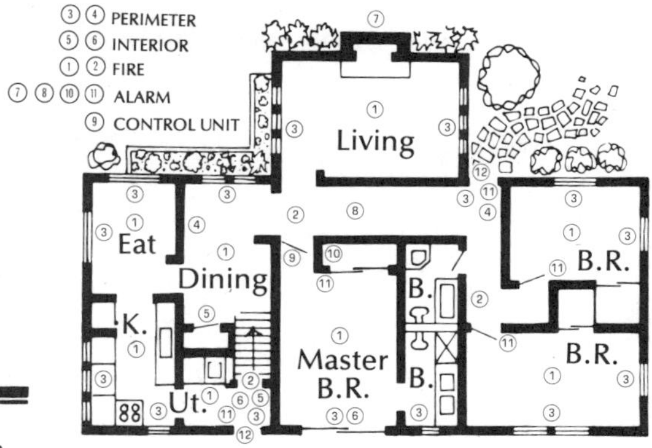

SECURITY SYSTEM PLANNING GUIDE

Intruder and Fire Detection System	Intruder Detection System	Fire Detection System	Components and Accessories
①		①	Heat Detectors in the middle of every room, including attic, basement and garage.
②		②	Smoke Detectors in passageways leading to bedrooms, at top of stairways.
③	③		Magnetic or Plunger Perimeter Detectors at every window and exterior door.
④	④		Infrared Detector to cover area of major traffic flow.
⑤	⑤		Magnetic or Plunger Interior Detectors at inside doors to basement, valuables closet.
⑥	⑥		Pressure Mats at exterior doors and stairways.
⑦	⑦	⑦	Outside Alarm on the highest point of the roof, under eaves.
⑧	⑧	⑧	Inside Alarm in central interior location to be clearly heard in all bedrooms with doors closed.
⑨	⑨	⑨	Control Unit in master bedroom or other convenient location.
⑩	⑩	⑩	Telephone Dialer in master bedroom, closet, etc.
⑪	⑪	⑪	Emergency Push Buttons at each exterior door and in each bedroom.
⑫	⑫		Exit/Entry Controls at main exterior doors.
NOT SHOWN			
			Foil Tape at every basement window.
			Radio Controls for hard-to-wire locations and at nearby detached buildings such as garage, barn, workshop.

To plan your home-security system, compare your residence to the one shown here. Using this chart you can determine appropriate applications for each type of sensing unit. Several companies offer control boxes with fire-only, intrusion-only or integrated fire and intrusion functions. By using integrated-function control boxes, you can build and modify a total protection system to meet your family's changing needs over the years. Ultrasonic or microwave area detectors provide alternatives to infrared or photoelectric beam units. Radio accessory units compromise the reliability of a hardwired system and should be shunted to allow selective use. Diagram is a sample only, a prescription for the "ideal" system.

REPRESENTATIVE WIRING DIAGRAM

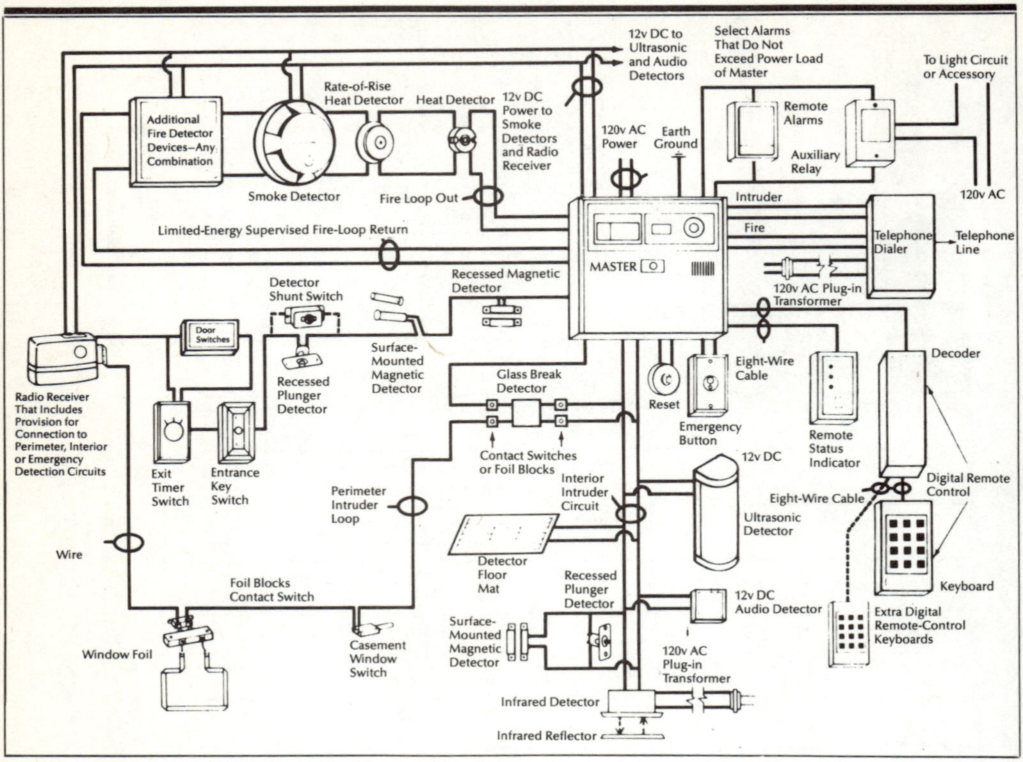

Here's one way comprehensive electronic home-security system could be wired. Note variety of sensors. Always refer to installation instructions for complete wiring information.

from the police. You need the goodwill of both to give your security measures credibility and effect. The simpler your system is, the more likely it will function to protect you—not imprison you.

CHOOSING COMPONENTS □ When you begin shopping around for components, keep in mind that there is probably as much good technology available to the do-it-yourselfer as there is to your not-so-handy or richer neighbors. As a do-it-yourselfer, stick to the simplest design, using the highest-quality components you can find.

Control box □ The heart of any system is the control box. Besides receiving an intrusion message from a sensor and signaling the alarm to sound, control boxes that monitor smoke and heat detectors are available. Honeywell, for example, makes a control box that even

Security Components

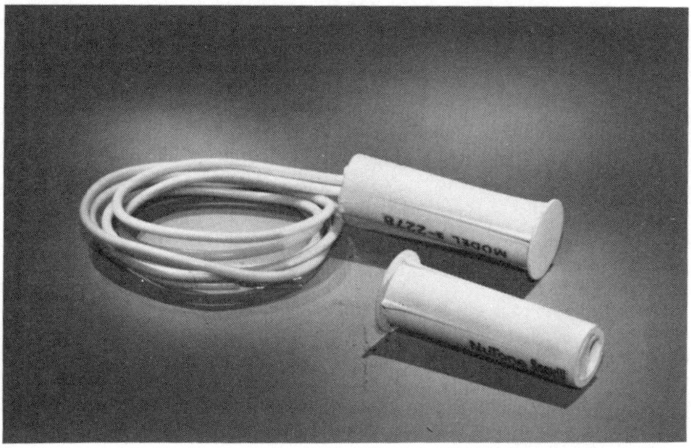

Basic magnetic sensor for use on window or door to detect unauthorized opening.

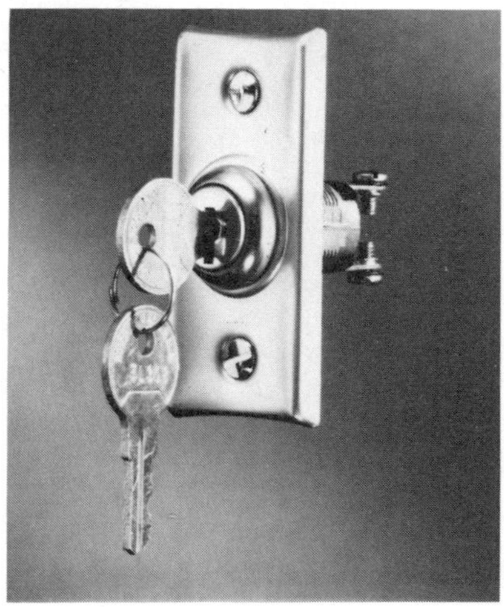

One type of alarm switch. Key helps reduce potential for unauthorized deployment or disengagement of system.

Photoelectric cell-type sensor can masquerade as electric outlet, providing area coverage.

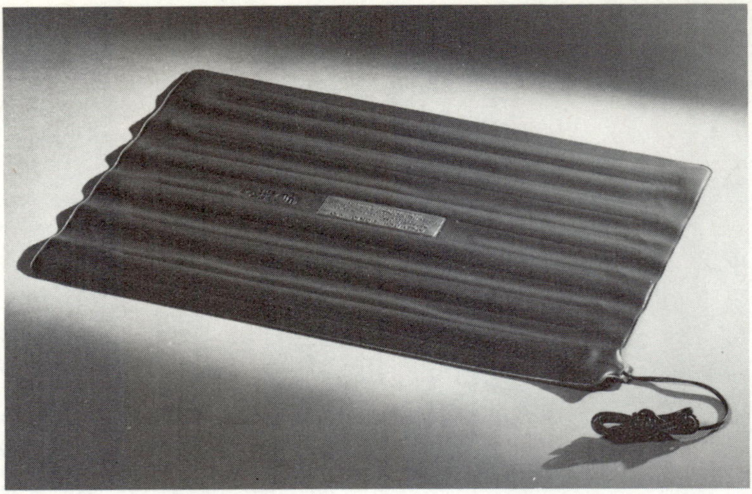

Pressure sensor is ideal for use along interior pathways leading to valuables; camouflage with scatter rug or carpeting.

Electronic horn out-performs bell in decibels, can be designed without moving parts.

Bell or horn alarm mounted outside house should be protected from tampering. This is what professionals would call a high-grade installation—no wires show anywhere.

Typical window-foil installation. Sensors that detect glass breaking are available which take the place of foil and are harder to defeat.

sounds house power, heating systems and medical alerts—more than just conveniences for families with one or more members suffering serious, chronic or high-risk coronary or respiratory conditions.

You can buy a control box that looks like a stereo receiver, masquerades as a book or tucks quietly away in a hall closet. The controls on the box should be simple and readable to all members of the family. Its design should allow you to easily add or remove features as your requirements change over the years. Central location and low visibility are important installation considerations, for obvious reasons.

Control boxes are available for fire detection only, fire and burglary detection in combination, and burglary detection only. Also available are one-box systems based on computer-monitored microwave technology which allow you to use your stereo speakers as alarms. Optional high-volume horns are available as alternatives to stereo speakers. They provide the advantage of being weatherproof, so you can mount them on the exterior of the house if you choose.

The control box is usually the single most expensive component, and even the thriftiest do-it-yourselfer should expect to plunk down at least $50 to $80 for this one item.

Sensors □ Sensors range from the simplest magnetic switches for use on doors and windows to ultrasophisticated microwave, infrared, ultrasonic and shock-detection equipment. In fact the only technology employed in commercial security systems not available to the homeowner—primarily due to cost and sensitivity—is capacitance measurement.

An effective system can be assembled for less than $200 using basic equipment and a ground-floor-opening strategy. A couple of zone sensors—either microwave or infrared—can cover areas where high-ticket, easily fenced valuables (stereo, color television, silverware, coin collections) are stored, thus beefing up your system at modest cost.

Alarms □ These are simple but easy-to-take-for-granted items. Alarms on the inside of the house may frighten intruders without necessarily warning the neighborhood. Alarms on the outside of the house may be spotted by burglars careful enough to case your home before they strike. Any part of your system the burglar spots in time can be evaded or defeated.

The features to look for in an alarm include decibel level and range; ease of mounting; provisions to conceal, armor or tamperproof the device; and distinctive, hard-to-ignore sound not likely to be mistaken for something it isn't. For externally mounted alarms, weatherproofing is also important—a wet alarm shorted out of commission obviously destroys the effectiveness of even the most sophisticated system.

Horns are much louder than bells, as well as much more expensive. While commercial establishments frequently invest in silent alarms, which ring only at police or monitor stations, this type of system is probably useless to the homeowner. Even an amateur burglar can clean out the typical house and make his escape in the time it takes police and an alarm company to respond to a silent alarm.

Accessories □ Among those available for home-security systems, the most useful by far is the telephone dialer (see page 144). While this component may run to $250 or more by itself, it gives a system immense flexibility. In combination with central-station service, private answering service or a direct line to police, it can provide 24-hour backup and is available both to the do-it-yourselfer and the alarm service customer.

Another useful (and for active families, probably necessary) accessory is the shunt switch, which allows you to turn off selected parts of your system. For example, you can switch off the rear-door sensor during a backyard barbecue that leaves the interior of the house unoccupied. You and your family have convenient access through the single entry under your direct surveillance, but you have an instantaneous warning if a burglar should try a daytime ripoff through any out-of-sight entry points.

TIPS ON INSTALLATION □ As noted earlier, you have three types of equipment to choose from: hardwired, wireless (or radio) and line-carrier. Miniatures and stand-alones often lack the sheer decibel power to really do the job. The popular door-mounted chainlock alarm can help. But its disadvantages include low decibel power and an interior mounting that turns the door into the baffle (or muffler), reducing the odds of someone outside the house recognizing the threat and calling the authorities.

However, smaller alarm kits are inexpensive. One burglar alarm kit from Trine Manufacturing, which costs about $20, comes with

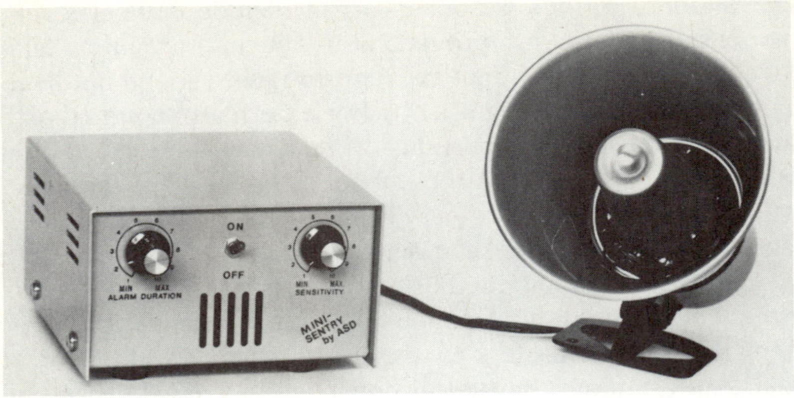

A stand-alone system with deafening decibel power, based on ultrasonic technology.

everything you need to protect a door or a window, including horn alarm, magnetic switches and wiring. The unit can be expanded, using additional magnetic switches and up to 150′ of wiring for greater perimeter protection.

To install this unit, first determine where you want to put the magnetic contact switch, magnet and master alarm. When used on a door, the magnet and switch are usually positioned at the top, above the handle or knob. The master alarm is located where it can't be seen or reached from outdoors. Wire from a switch to the master alarm is concealed along the moldings or on the sides of either windows or doors. Excess wiring can be either wound around the inner posts of the alarm station or cut off to desired length.

Many companies offer a choice between wired and wireless systems. Line-carrier components plug into the wall sockets of your home's electrical system and use that circuitry to carry the alarm signal to the alarm box.

Except for concealing the wire, assembling your own hardwired home-security system can be compared to hooking up a component stereo system. But that "except" is important. To maximize the effectiveness of your system, you need to achieve the highest-grade installation possible. The better the installation, the less visible and therefore the less vulnerable the system. The simplest strategy is to run all the wiring through either the basement or the attic. The basement is preferable if it's unfinished, because the distance you'll

WIRING DIAGRAM

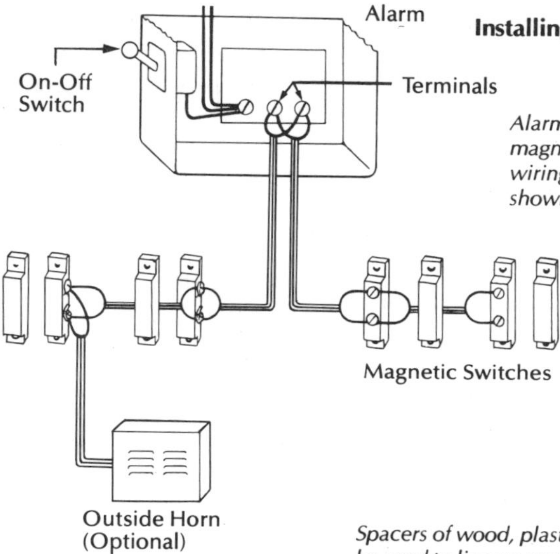

Installing Low-Cost Hardwired Kit

Alarm kit from Trine Mfg. includes magnetic switch assembly, alarm and wiring for about $20. System is wired as shown here.

Spacers of wood, plastic or cardboard can be used to line up magnet and switch.

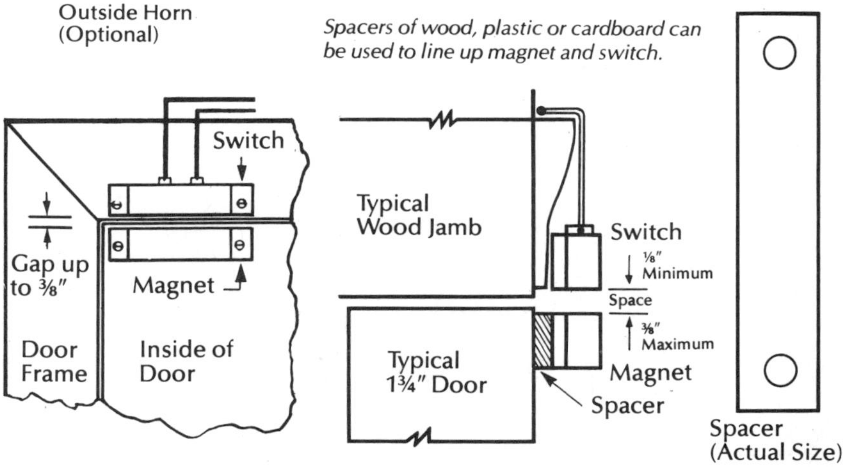

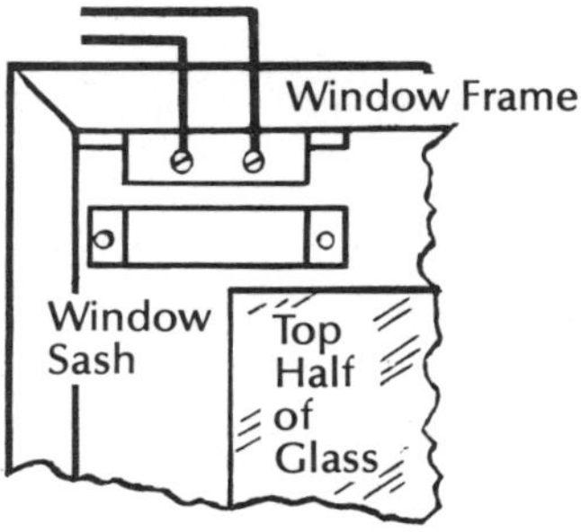

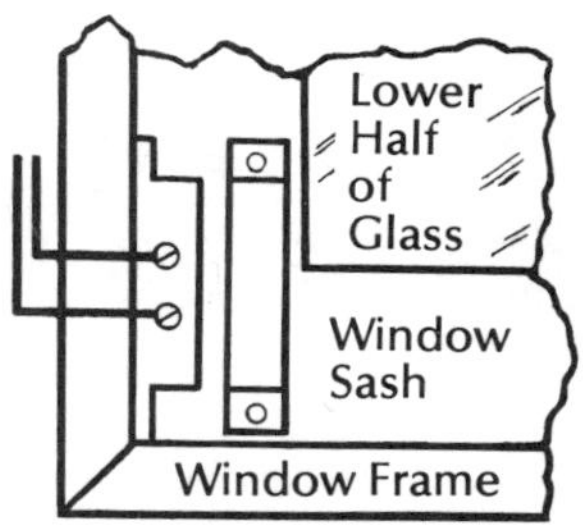

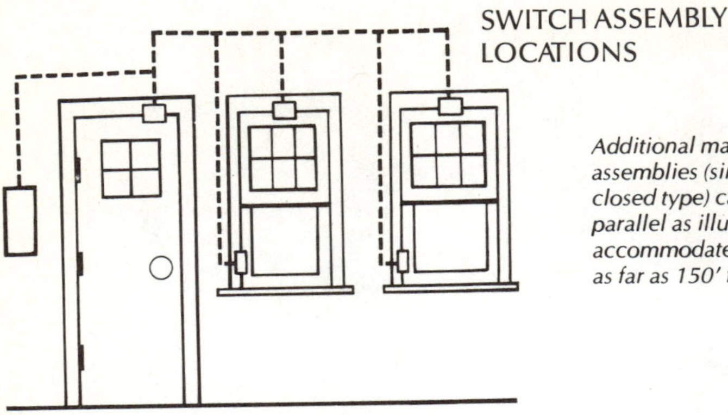

Additional magnetic switch assemblies (single-pole, normally closed type) can be wired in parallel as illustrated. This kit accommodates additional switches as far as 150′ from master alarm.

have to run wire between floors is shorter. You'll probably need to put sensors on the basement doors and windows anyway.

The tools required vary somewhat with the equipment you buy. A complete tool kit might contain a short wire fish, a small power drill, screwdrivers, a soldering iron, a socket wrench and sockets, wire cutters, stud locator, horseshoe nails, silicone cement, plaster and plastic wood.

Home-security systems are available prepackaged. This receiver is part of a Sears system which gives your home 24-hour fire and intrusion protection at a cost of $150 to $500, depending on the level of protection you want.

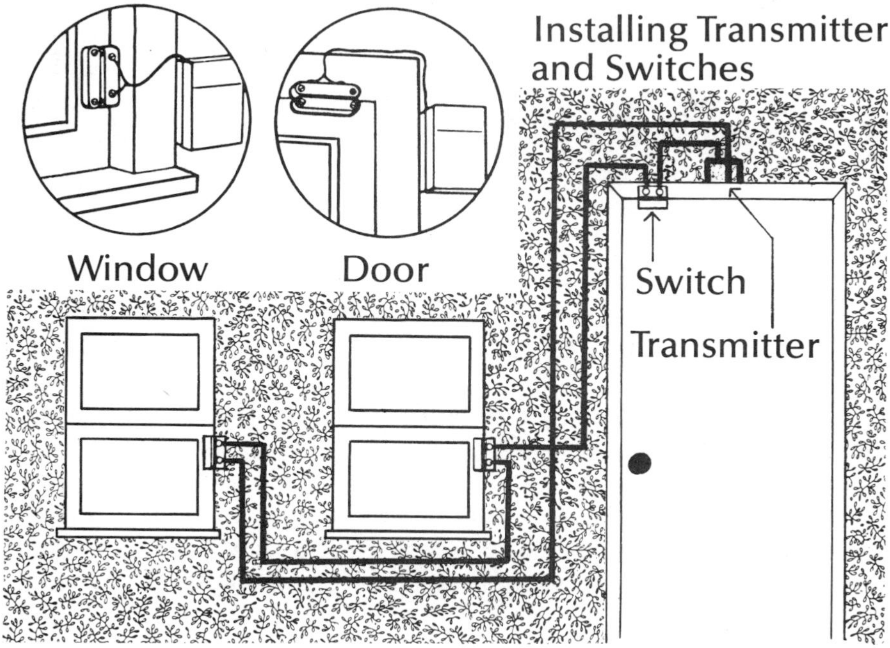

Only wiring necessary with this system is from transmitter, which signals receiver, to reed-type magnetic switches, using wire in kit. Single transmitter can service up to five switches. Rarer situations may require some ingenuity. When in doubt, pretest unusual installations before drilling holes in walls or door and window finishes.

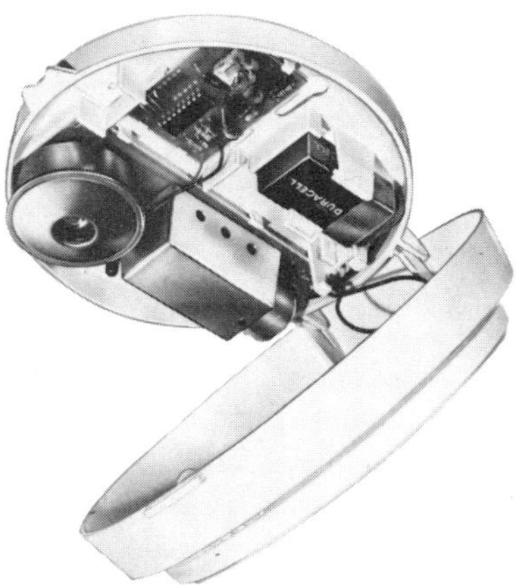

Smoke detector with built-in transmitter can send signal to transceiver, which sounds emergency warning. Outside horn, battery pack and phone dialer are other alarm-system options.

The major work involved is in the drilling of holes to receive recessed-type magnetic sensors, and punching through each door or window frame to run wire through to the basement or attic circuit. A wire fish is preferred for working wire among studs. Where the distances between entry and exit points for the wire are short, a coat hanger can also be fashioned into a perfectly usable wiring guide. Electricians use 5″ bits and run wire down the drill in order to reach the exit point.

The control box can be located in the basement stairwell. For your own convenience you should shunt the circuit with a key-activated safety switch, permitting you and your family to enter the house without setting off the alarm. Be sure your control box has an auxiliary power supply and an automatic conversion feature so if the AC current in your house fails, the backup DC power supply is brought into play.

If you mount an alarm on the outside of your home, be sure no wiring is exposed. Also be sure to tamper-proof the siren or bell box so that any attempt to disconnect it will set it off. Windows may require double sets of sensors—one set to cover the closed position, another to cover the open position. Remember to think of double-hung windows and Dutch doors as multiple entry points. But don't overdo the sensor bit. Remember, it's your house, not a jail.

If you choose to install your hardwired system on a lesser basis, you can still achieve a minimum level of concealment by running all wires along baseboards and over door frames, reducing the unsightliness and hazard of random wire.

Installing Hardwired System

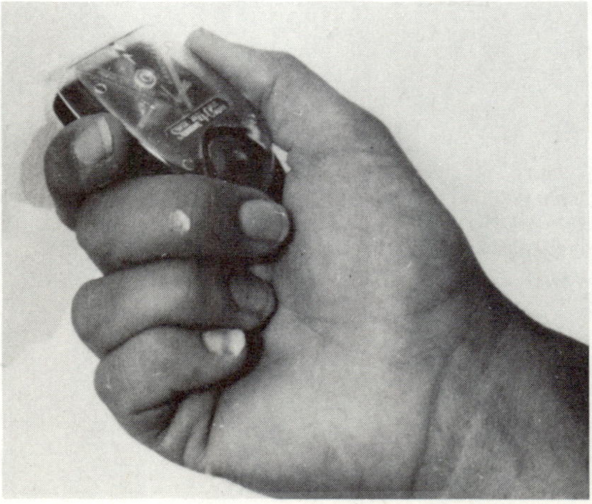

Stud locater finds spaces between structural members to help you decide where to put control box.

Mark control box location. It should be convenient to get to but concealed from view of strangers. Score sheetrock carefully and neatly; use level to true up all lines.

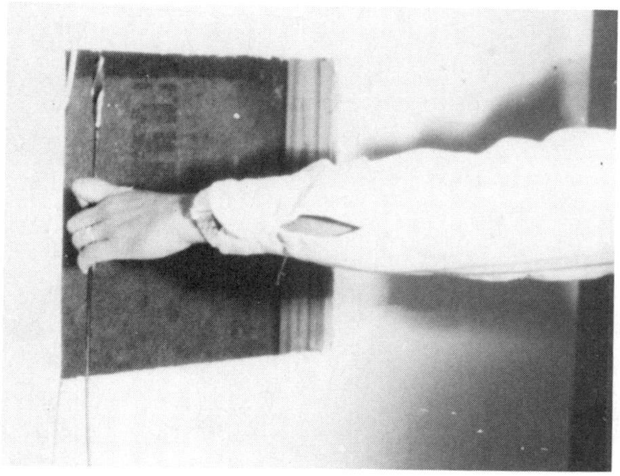

Once control box location has been prepared, start running lines from sensor locations to control box opening.

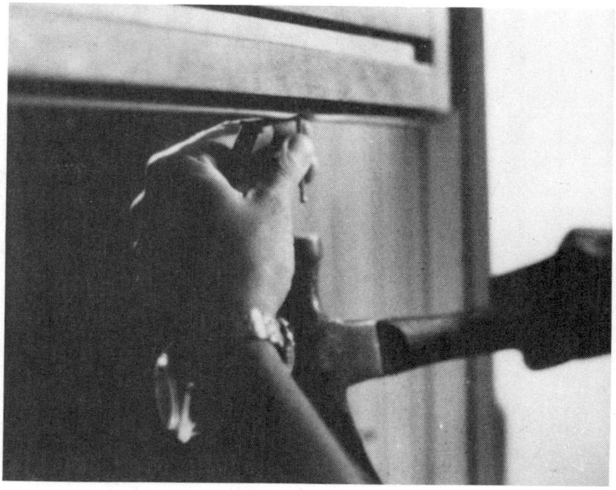

To align parts of recessed magnetic switch, hammer a nail into frame where magnetic actuator will go, and drop window. Nail mark on sill will be switch location.

Drill pilot hole before using flexible bit. Keep drill angled to compensate for angle of sill.

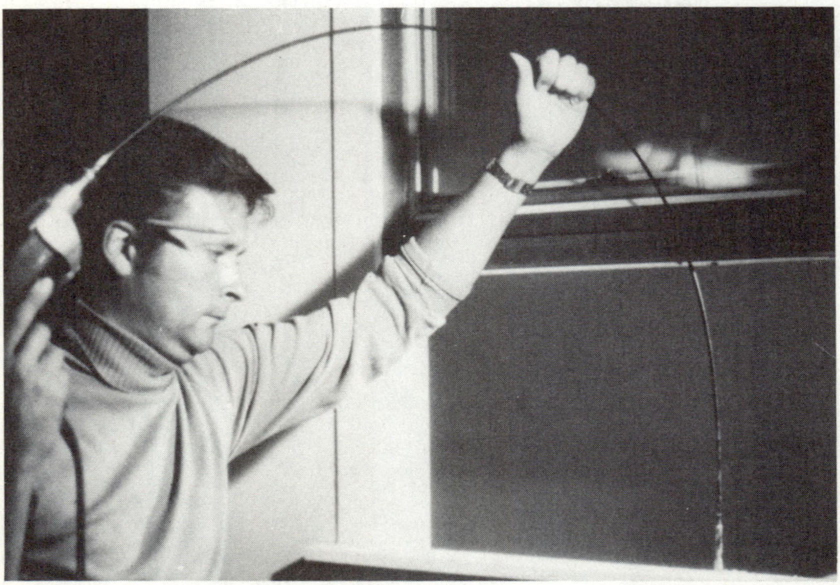

Flexible drill bit is invaluable aid to installation; works through in-the-wall obstructions like firebreaks.

Fishing wire goes through walls more quickly if you use wire trap. Start with a 4" or 5" loop of hard-drawn copper wire; form three loops of equal size.

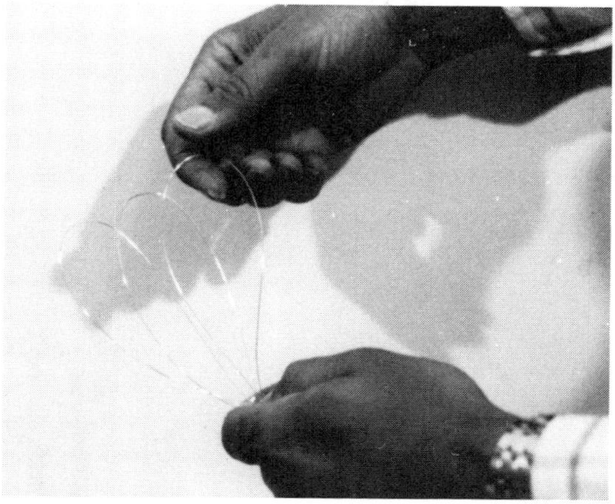

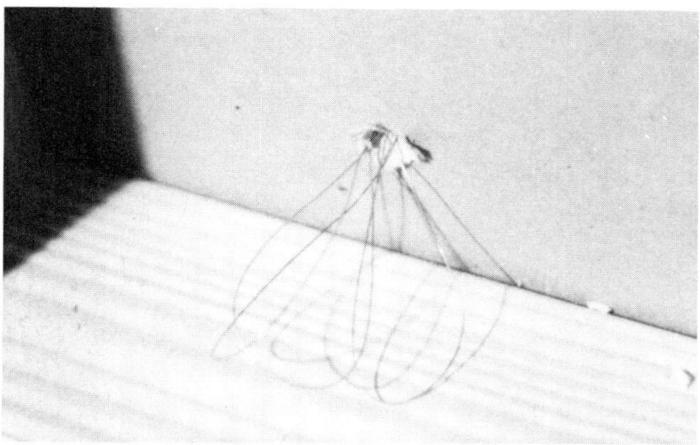

Force copper wire through wall.

From other end, work electrical snake down to wire and take three to four times on it.

Splice alarm wire to trap. Half-turn of snake should be enough to free any snags while working wire through wall.

Use only round-headed staples for securing wire; standard staples will crimp or short wire.

To put foil on window, first clean window with alcohol. Use square of wood or plexiglass to help draw foil pattern on outside of glass.

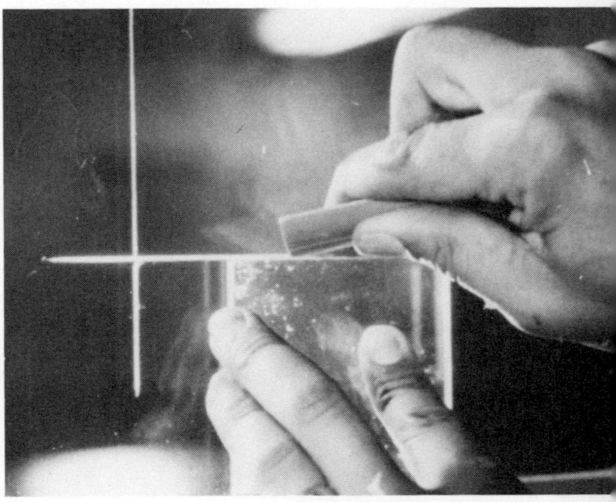

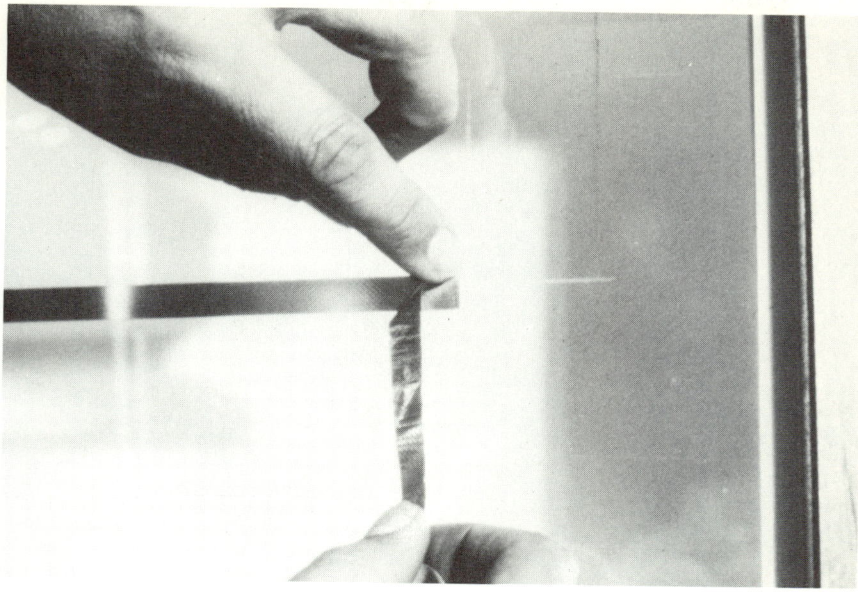

Be sure to stretch foil tightly. Corners must be creased, then folded in order to maintain good contact all around foil loop. After reinforcing each corner, continue to follow foil guide back to contact switch.

To install plunger switch at door, drill pilot hole, then use flexible bit as fish to run out wire.

Chisel out recess for plunger switch backplate.

Connect wire, and mount and secure switch.

Be sure to locate a panic button in your bedroom. This way you can use the system to drive off an intruder even when you're home. Panic buttons in other parts of the house may also be advisable—it's up to you.

A digital disarming device whose code is known only to members of your family can be mounted on the exterior of the house, reducing the possibility of your entering the house without remembering to disarm the system. This accessory prevents having to come up with apologies for disgruntled police.

If you'd like to read more, Radio Shack prints a booklet available from any of their stores for $1.50, entitled *Security for Your Home,* by Forrest Mims. John E. Cunningham has two books available from Howard W. Sams & Co.: *Electronic Intrusion Alarms* and *Security Electronics.*

Thief-Proofing Vehicles and Garages

CHAPTER 13 ■ Car theft is a $1.6 billion-a-year business, and even if your car is not stolen, you're picking up the tab through higher insurance premiums.

On a national average, 446 cars are stolen per 100,000 population. The average cost for auto-theft insurance is about $29 per year. But if you live in a major city you are paying far above that rate for theft coverage. In Chicago, for example, the average is about $150. In New York it's close to $275. In Boston, with more than 1,600 cars stolen per 100,000 population, you pay $300.

The FBI estimates that two-thirds of all auto thefts are committed by amateurs, and only one-third by professionals. Nearly two-thirds of all auto thefts could be prevented if the owners of the automobiles would take precautionary measures such as the ones outlined in this chapter.

HOW CARS ARE STOLEN

■ Not all cars are stolen for profit. One-third of all stolen cars are taken for joyrides. While the majority of these cars are recovered when abandoned by the joyrider, most are damaged or stripped of easily removed parts.

The next category of car thief is the amateur. He is probably an opportunist who will steal cars that are highly vulnerable. He won't go to great pains to steal your car, but if you extend him an invitation by leaving the keys in the car, parking it on a dark street or forgetting to lock it, he'll take advantage of your carelessness.

The pro who wants your car will find a way to take it. He

knows how most simple alarm systems are wired, and he'll disconnect the alarm.

Honest people make the mistake of believing that all others are honest, too. It has been estimated that four out of ten cars stolen are taken by pros who operate in unmarked tow trucks; they simply hook onto a car and haul it away. Often the cars are transported in broad daylight from crowded areas such as sports stadiums or shopping centers. Onlookers believe that your car is being hauled for a parking violation or at your request.

Pros cruise to "shop" for an auto that has been "ordered" by a client or will bring a good price. Likely targets include expensive American cars such as Corvettes, Lincolns or Cadillacs. Also high on the most-wanted list are expensive foreign makes. Sharp, new, loaded cars equipped with fancy wheels, radial tires, tape decks and the like are also targets. Even junkers may be stolen for parts, but most thieves follow the dictum "never steal anything small."

Since the car thief may get 10% of the value of the car for stealing it for a "client," he may go to great lengths to steal your car. You may be fingered by someone as owning the car in question. The thief may learn your habits, job location and where you shop so he can steal your car when he is least likely to be apprehended. If you park once a week on the dark side of your club, a bar or bowling alley, or leave your car on the street, that's the time the pro will choose. He needs less than one minute to enter the car and drive it away.

The pro operates in the evening, often between 8 and 10 P.M. He has the advantages of darkness and a lot of activity by the public. He'll avoid working after midnight because neighbors and police are more suspicious of activity at that hour.

If your car is left in a vulnerable spot, it takes only seconds to steal it. A device called a slim-jim is slipped inside the door frame and the lock is tripped. Once in, the thief will knock off the chrome ring around your ignition lock, use a slide-hammer (a body repairman's tool) to pull out the ignition, start the car with a screwdriver and drive away.

COMMON-SENSE PRECAUTIONS

■ There is little you can do to be absolutely sure some pro won't steal your car. But you can take elementary precautions that could reduce your chances of theft by at least 50%.

Always lock your car and take the keys. In Boston a "Lock Your

Car'' campaign cut auto theft by 48% in a two-year period. According to a 1978 report from the New York State Senate Committee on Transportation, 40% of all cars stolen had keys left in them by careless owners. Half of that 40% had the keys in the ignition, and half had keys ''hidden'' under the car seat or behind the sun visor.

Avoid parking in lots where you must leave the keys with an attendant. It's a simple matter to make a wax impression of your keys, and the car can then be picked up at the culprit's convenience. For the same reason, if you must park where the keys are to be left, keep only the ignition key available. Keys to your home, garage and other cars can be duplicated by a dishonest attendant, and your home ''visited'' later.

Avoid parking on poorly lit streets. If you must park on the street try to park near or under a streetlight. When you're at home, don't leave the car parked in the drive overnight. If you garage the car it will be out of sight, and a thief will have to break into the garage to get the car.

Accessory items such as tape decks, CB radios or fancy wheel covers may make your car the target of the thief who steals cars to strip them of parts. If you often park in areas where the car is vulnerable to thieves, consider passing up these expensive options. Also, a car in which luggage, cameras or other personal items are visible may encourage a thief to steal the car. Take time to place your personal items out of sight in your car's trunk.

Fit out your car with antitheft equipment such as a siren alarm or a device that renders the electrical system inoperable.

ANTITHEFT DEVICES

■ Some car-theft rings will load your car onto a trailer and haul it away to be sold or stripped. Others use tow trucks. Alarms that assume the car will be driven away under its own power will not deter this kind of theft.

However, there are a number of devices you can use to deter the joyrider and the amateur thief. A thief can gain entry to many cars simply by bending a clothes hanger into a hook, passing the wire in through the crack around the door or window, hooking the door lock knob with the loop and pulling it upward. A number of door lock knobs are available that either disappear into boots or have no knob on the end, so they can't be hooked with a wire. These replacement knobs cost approximately $1.50 per door, and are easily installed.

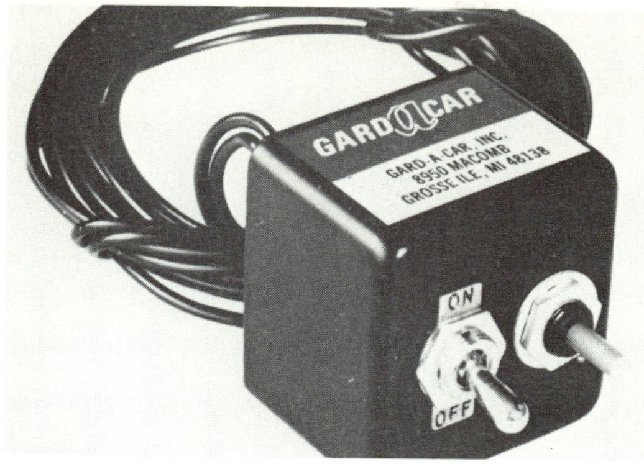

Vehicle Antitheft Devices

This device installs in minutes by connecting two wires. If thief starts car, engine will stall in less than eight seconds.

Small transmitter installed in vehicle sends out coded radio signal which is received by pocket page similar to those carried by doctors. Silent alarm signal range is over a half-mile.

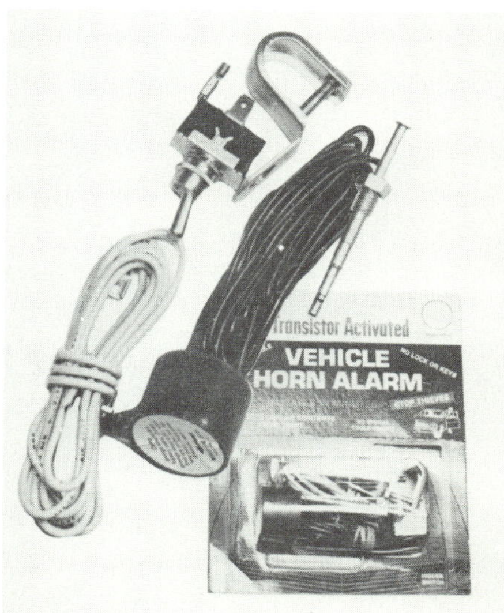

This low-cost horn alarm for cars, trucks or recreational vehicles sounds vehicle horn if light-equipped door, hood, trunk or any other electrical accessory is activated. Installs with screwdriver and pliers.

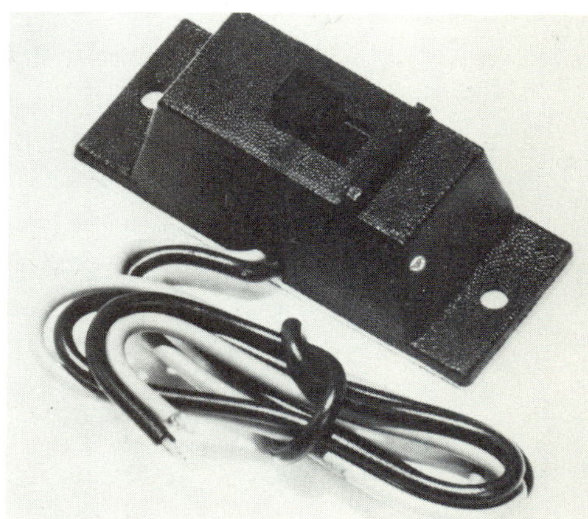

This unit creates effect of flooded carburetor. Confuses would-be thieves by allowing starter to operate normally but preventing engine from being started. Attaches without drilling or splicing wires.

This patented door lock knob makes it difficult for thief to get inside car. When knob is up, it operates like other locks; when down, prevents use of hook to unlock vehicle.

You also can buy steering-wheel locks. These are heavy-duty metal or plastic yokes which clamp the steering wheel into a set position. In addition, you can buy electrical or mechanical devices that defeat a thief's efforts to start a car, or cause it to stall immediately after starting. And you can buy alarms that emit a piercing noise which will drive the thief away.

Some alarms sound when the thief tries to start the engine; others can be installed to sound if anyone tampers with the car doors or trunk lid, or if the car is moved slightly. Some have pagers that alert you that someone is tampering with the car even when you are away from the vehicle. Alarms can protect the engine compartment, trunk, door or the entire vehicle.

Though not for the average do-it-yourselfer, sophisticated alarms installed by professionals will protect all entry points into the vehicle, and will even sound if someone jacks the car up to remove wheels. These can be hand actuated while you're driving. If, for example, someone attempted to stop you on a deserted street, you would just hit the switch and the alarm would sound like the European-type police siren.

A low-cost (about $10) auto alarm that triggers the horn should be a satisfactory discouragement for the amateur and semipro. The horn-triggering device, made for under-hood installation, contains a pendulum with a sensitivity adjustment. If an attempt to open the hood or a front door makes the car shake, the pendulum swings and completes a circuit as if the horn button had been pressed. After 10 to 15 seconds the pendulum disengages and the horn-blowing stops.

The pendulum system is wired through an off-on switch which is hidden somewhere you can reach from outside, such as between the grille and radiator. This permits you to lock up without setting off the horn. The installation shown in the illustrations isn't difficult.

If you don't know how to find the horn relay to which the device is wired, here's one approach: 1) locate the horn by having a helper press the horn button; 2) disconnect the wire from the horn terminal;

Installing Auto Burglar Alarm

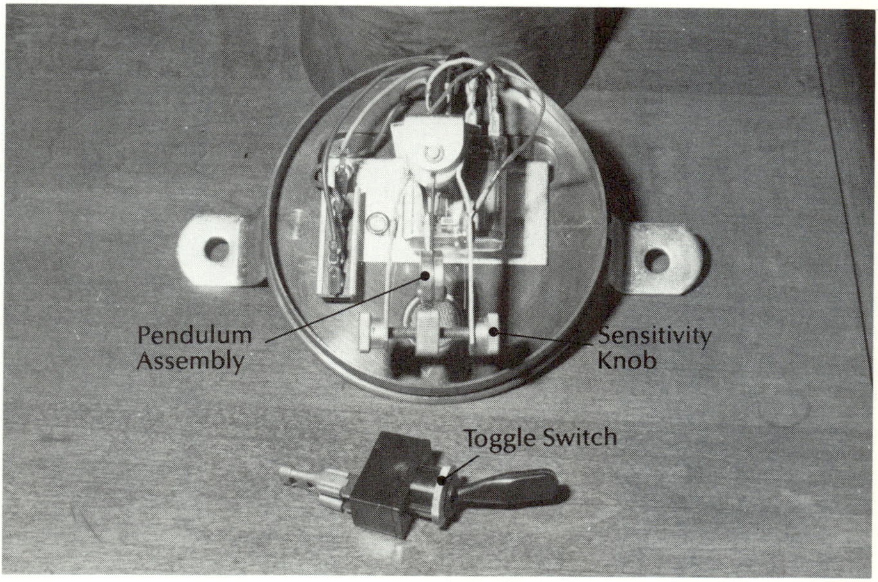

Closeup look at one pendulum device. Turning knurled screw at bottom right sets sensitivity. After installation of device is complete, turn screw as required so horn blows if attempt is made to lift hood or open front door.

Pendulum must be mounted so it swings across car from driver's to passenger's side. On this particular car, only available space was on sheet metal on passenger's side of radiator. On other cars you may be able to mount it on the firewall.

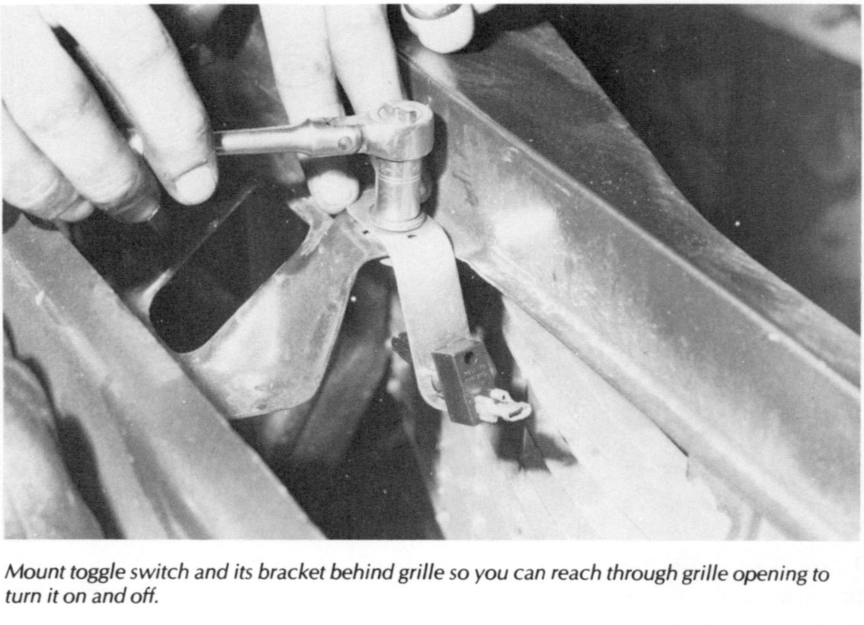

Mount toggle switch and its bracket behind grille so you can reach through grille opening to turn it on and off.

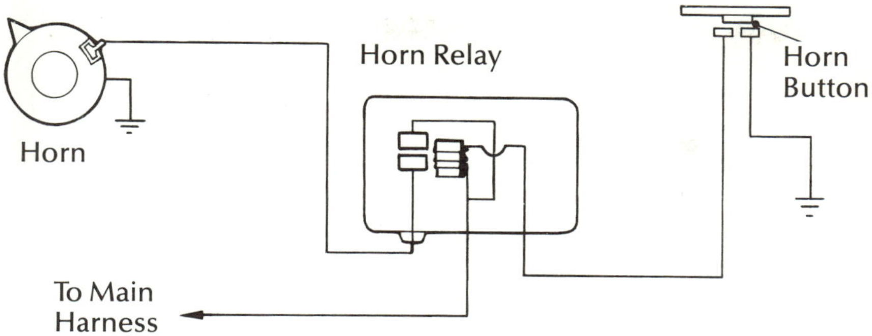

Typical schematic for horn circuit. When you press horn button, you complete circuit through relay, which closes and allows current to flow to horn. Horn button provides electrical ground for relay, just as pendulum device does when activated.

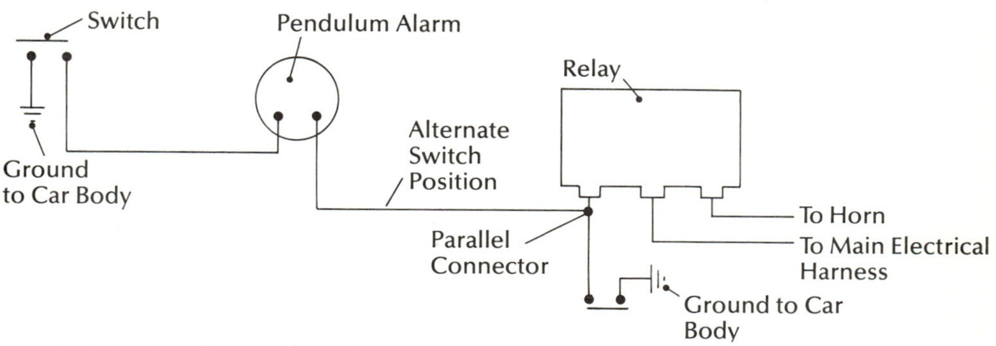

Typical wiring schematic for pendulum alarm system. If pendulum alarm is self-grounding (e.g., through mounting bolts), switch is spliced into wire between horn relay and pendulum alarm, as indicated by "alternate switch position."

3) have the helper press the horn button until you hear a clicking from the horn relay; and 4) trace the click to the relay, a small canister usually under the dash. It will have three terminals. The "2" or "S" terminal is the one you want.

To give a potential thief a harder time, you can take an additional step. Mount a second switch (an inexpensive item available at auto supply stores) in a more obvious location than the first. Run wires from it, but don't bother to connect them. Just tuck them under somewhere, or you'll have two switches to remember to turn both on and off. If the thief comes back for a second try after the horn has stopped blowing, he may flip that dummy switch and think the alarm is off. When the horn blows again, he'll probably give up.

For many owners of late-model cars with steering-column locks, equipment under the hood or in the trunk—a $60 battery, $100 alternator, $200 electronic ignition distributor and other easy-to-remove, expensive parts—is in danger of theft.

If you want only under-hood protection or wish to add trunk coverage to your alarm system, install a normally closed spring-loaded plunger switch, such as the door-jamb switch that turns on the dome light. This switch, available in auto supply stores, can be mounted under the hood so that when the hood is closed, the switch is pushed open. A similar installation can be made at the trunk compartment.

When properly wired through a second switch hidden in the passenger compartment, this circuit can be activated before you lock up, and it will sound the horn if an attempt is made to open the hood or trunk-compartment lid. With this arrangement, the horn will sound until the hood or lid is closed, which poses the danger of a dead battery when you return. However, you probably will have scared off a thief, and you'll have saved a lot more than the cost of the battery boost-start you'll need.

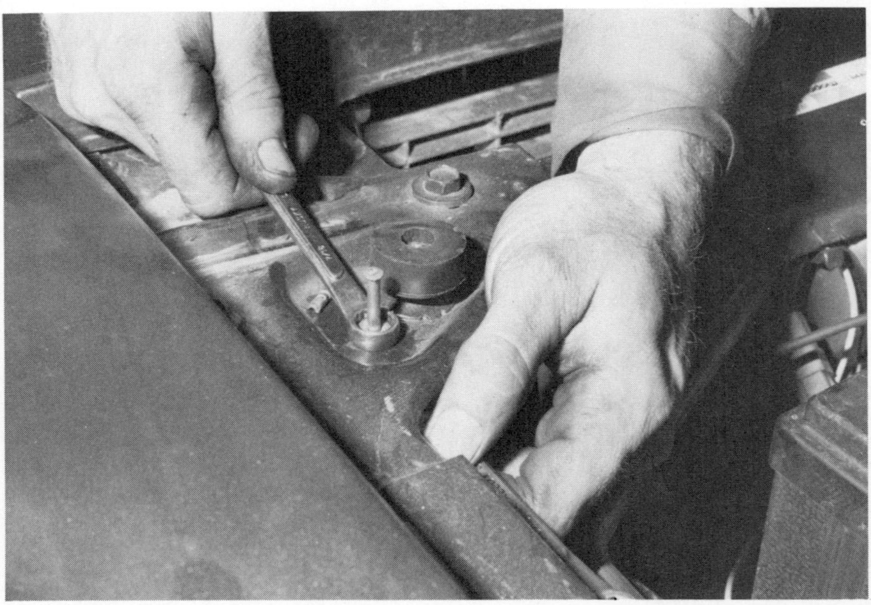

Installing door-jamb switch on engine-compartment front sheet metal. Switch is installed so that when hood is closed, switch plunger is pushed down, opening normally closed switch.

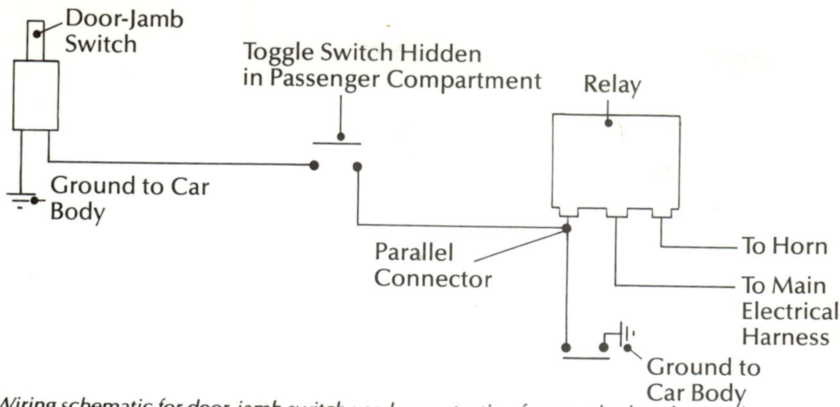

Wiring schematic for door-jamb switch used as protection from under-hood or trunk-compartment theft.

VEHICLE IDENTIFICATION □ A unique vehicle identification system called Identicar is now available through many auto glass shops. A permanent computer-selected code is engraved into every piece of glass on the vehicle. The code, which can't be altered or removed without total glass replacement, consists of 3/8″-high letters, which become your vehicle's fingerprints. All codes, plus the vehicle's description, owner's name and vehicle identification number, are maintained in a national registry.

The information is available to law-enforcement agencies via a nationwide toll-free phone line. Besides deterring theft, the code facilitates the recovery and identification process if the auto is stolen. The Identicar code can also be used for recreational vehicles,

Code is engraved in glass while you wait and can't be removed without replacement of every piece of glass in the vehicle.

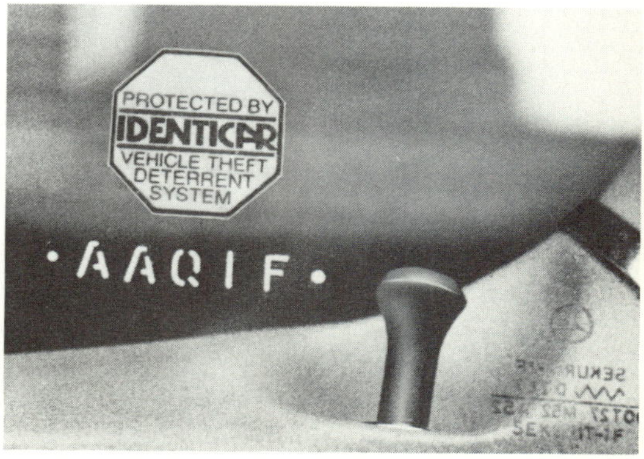

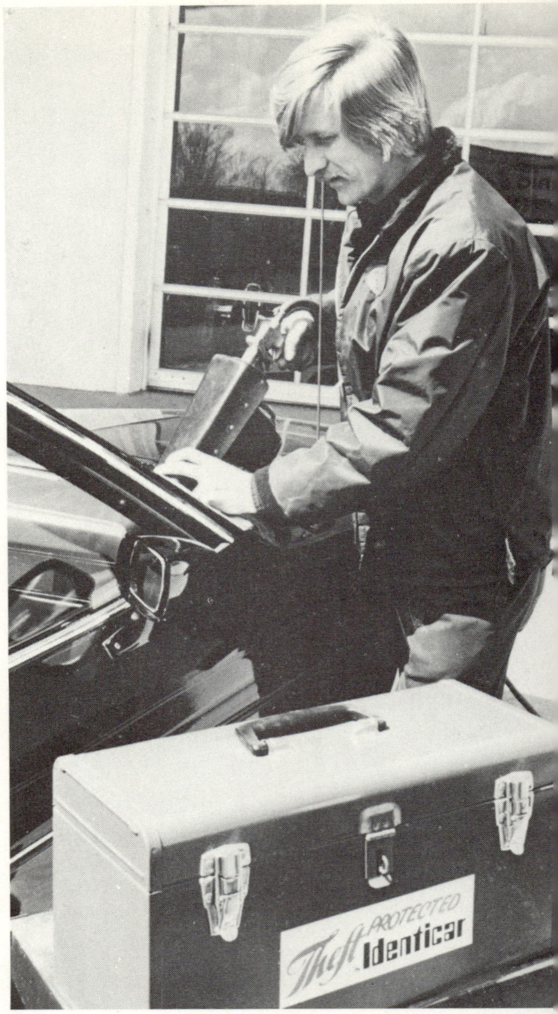

After code is engraved, it is registered and data is available to law-enforcement agencies.

boats or any other vehicle that has windows. The system is simple and inexpensive, and can be installed while you wait. An Identicar decal is also placed on the glass so the thief will know your car is marked and will be more likely to pass it up.

IF IT'S STOLEN

■ Suppose you find the car gone one day, in spite of all your precautions. What to do? First consider the possibilities. Are you sure the car was stolen? If the car was taken by a friend or relative, reporting it stolen could have tragic consequences. Police officers are understandably wary of approaching a car when they believe the driver is a thief, and might shoot suspected auto thieves they think are attempting to evade arrest. Also, if you are behind on your car payments, financial institutions sometimes "steal" the car, taking it without notifying you.

If you're sure someone you know or your finance company did not take the car, report it stolen immediately. Keep your license number and auto identification number handy. Report the license number, make, model and color of the car in your phone call to police. If your car was stolen by professionals, a swift report and pickup order may be your only hope of recovering the car. It may also help police if you have a color photo of the car.

As soon as you've notified police, call your insurance agent. Auto policies generally cover car rental or a portion of the car rental if your car is stolen (usually $10 a day). However, most companies will not pay for the first 48 hours. The quicker you make your report to the insurance company, the quicker your rental provision will go into effect.

Even though your car loss may be paid in part by the insurance company, it's doubtful that insurance will cover the entire replacement value of your car. Keep in mind, too, that you may be open to a possible lawsuit by a third party should the thief damage property or injure someone while operating your vehicle. Leaving your keys in the car may lead a court to conclude that your negligence made the damage or injury possible. Lock your car and take the keys.

Because the insurance company is liable for the value of the car and obliged to pay a fee for car rental until your case is settled, payment will usually be made in 30 days or less. They will not wait until the car is recovered. Payment for the car is generally based on blue book value (the average retail price), and title to the car goes to the insurance company. It's important that you retain receipts showing the cost of the car and of any expensive options that you have had installed. If you have recently put in air conditioning, a new set of radial tires or other costly items, you may be reimbursed for them.

DRIVING PROTECTION

- Although a CB radio is often the target of thieves, it can be a comforting device if you drive at night or travel in unfamiliar areas.

The CB keeps you constantly in touch with others, and you can put out a call for help if you are harrassed by hoodlums or your car becomes disabled. To avoid loss of the radio itself, buy the type that slides out of its clamps and has a magnetic antenna. Both units can be concealed in the car trunk or taken into the home when they are not in use.

Keep your car doors locked while driving, and keep your car in good repair. Having a car in sound running condition with good tires greatly reduces your chances of a breakdown and subsequently being stranded. Keep an eye on the gas gauge. It's a good practice to have the gas tank filled when the gauge shows a quarter tank. Your best defense is common sense: Avoid situations that increase your exposure to dangerous confrontations.

RECREATIONAL EQUIPMENT

■ Recreational vehicles (RVs) and boats offer a tempting target to the thief for several reasons. They often contain expensive equipment that can be lifted—CB radios, stereos, refrigerators and the like. Also, RVs suggest people on vacation or an outing. They may contain valuable cameras, luggage, guns, fishing or other sporting equipment.

RVs can be protected with alarms or ignition interruption devices, or the windows can be etched with Identicar codes. Beyond the precautions mentioned for cars, you might take the RV to an auto body shop and have the storage-locker and entry locks upgraded. It's also a simple matter to remove the coil wire, or the rotor from the distributor of an engine. You can then be sure your auto or RV can't be started. If you are leaving your boat docked overnight, remove the plug wires or coil wire and place them in your tackle box so the motor can't be started.

ATTACHED GARAGES

■ The attached garage offers easy access to most homes. Often the garage doors and locks are of poor quality, so there is no challenge to getting through them. Once in, the burglar can steal the car or whatever is in the garage. This offers a tempting scenario for the criminal: vulnerability, concealment, convenient access.

The burglar can pull into your drive, open the garage door, back his own vehicle inside and close the door. He can now loot your

Garage door opener can be a significant security measure as well as a convenience, particularly if your garage is attached directly to your home. By eliminating the walk between garage and car, the radio-controlled garage door opener reduces your vulnerability to mugging. It's also one of the least expensive projects you can undertake—using hammer, pliers, wrench, drill and a pair of screwdrivers (standard and Phillips), you'll have it installed in a matter of hours.

home or garage at his leisure. If you have a garage workshop, he can use your tools to force entry into the house, or steal the tools.

You can do a lot to beef up garage doors and the service door between the house and garage. For example, you can replace cheap hollow-core doors with solid wood or insulated steel doors. You can add a strong deadbolt lock above a key-in-the-knob lock on the service door. You can secure garage windows as you would those in the rest of your house.

Consider relocating your garage workshop. If you have no other space available, at least remove the more valuable tools to a safer spot during long absences from home. Mark your power tools with identification numbers, just as you would other valuables. As added protection, put a heavy-duty security padlock through the track of the garage door so it can't be opened.

Upgrade the door with a radio-controlled opener. Installation of a garage door opener is a fairly simple task for the handyman. Most openers will contain a set of instructions in the parts package.

The automatic opener will make your garage more secure because it's impossible to raise the door without the electronic control unit. It will also serve to increase your personal safety by enabling you to open the garage door, drive into a lighted garage and close the door without leaving your car. The light that comes on automatically when you press the button to open the door will stay on for a short time so you can see to open the house door and go inside. Then the light will go off.

WORK AGAINST THIEVES

■ There are a number of things you can do to make it more difficult for auto thieves to operate. At the state level, you can urge elected officials to adopt the recommendations made by a New York legislative committee for putting identification numbers on car parts most often stripped. You can work to have businesses that sell or scrap cars licensed and required to keep accurate records of all transactions.

At the national level, you can demand legislation to compel automakers to put better locks on all doors; to make antitheft devices standard equipment; to stamp the vehicle identification number on the engine, transmission and other expensive components in addition to placing the number on the auto body; and to make locks for hood and trunk that can be activated from inside the vehicle.

These steps would add to the cost of the vehicle. But they would drastically drop the rate at which cars are stolen, saving the consumer $1.6 billion per year.

Pointers on Personal Protection

CHAPTER 14 ■ The preceding chapters show you some of the do-it-yourself measures you can use to boost the level of your home's security. There are a number of steps you can take to further ensure your personal safety, both inside your home and while you're away.

If your home is burglarized while you're out, don't panic. Upon returning, if you see an open window, broken glass or door ajar—or any other evidence of entry—don't go into the house. Find a phone and call the police. If you discover your home is being burglarized while you and family are in it, the best procedure is to keep calm and, for your personal safety, don't confront the burglar directly.

Most burglars are young. In a recent year, 77% of all persons arrested for robbery were under the age of 25; 58% were under 21. Most are unarmed, and few intentionally enter an occupied building. Ordinarily the burglar's only desire after being discovered is to escape as fast as he can.

Don't try to apprehend a criminal. If you can, observe enough about him to identify him later for police. But don't endanger yourself and family trying to be a hero. Calmly stay put and don't interfere with his attempt to make a hasty exit.

Many authorities urge you not to do anything provocative if you experience a direct confrontation with an intruder, who may be carrying a weapon. If circumstances bring you face to face, the only "weapon" you will have is psychology. Try to maintain eye contact with the intruder, keep a conversation going and cooperate as far as you can. Doing so will increase your chances of survival. But keep in mind that the art of negotiating with an armed, desperate criminal requires intensive training and skill which the average homeowner lacks.

HOMEOWNER WEAPONS

■ A number of personal protection devices are available to the homeowner, including whistles, horns, pressurized tear gas and, of course, firearms. Firearms are considered by many homeowners to be the ultimate in self-defense. But most law-enforcement agencies disagree. The overriding consensus of these authorities is that unless you are well trained in the use of such weapons and are fully aware of the legal implications of shooting an intruder, you are much better off not using a firearm to protect your home and property.

Incidents where a homeowner mistakenly injures a friend or relative are common. Also, laws governing ownership and use of firearms vary across the country. If you have firearms in your home with the idea that you will use them to protect your property, make sure you know how the law is interpreted and enforced in your area.

If you store firearms at home, take steps to prevent the possibility of hurting the innocent. Gun accidents take over 2,000 lives a year in this country. Especially weigh the danger of keeping firearms in your home if you have children. If you must have firearms, make sure they are safely locked up and protected. Various keyed locks are available for rifles, revolvers and shotguns which lock the trigger so the gun can't be fired. Keep firearms separate from ammunition supplies.

DEALING WITH STRANGERS

■ Various devices from door peepholes to closed-circuit TV systems are available to help you identify callers before allowing them into your home. Be cautious with repairmen, deliverymen, fund-raisers, real-estate salesmen or other solicitors. They may be burglars posing as someone else in order to case your home.

The task of evaluating strangers who come to your home is one you can't afford to take lightly. Handling strangers who come to your door begins with identification. Demand it. If you are not familiar with the type of identification offered, look up the phone number of the organization the stranger claims to represent, and call to verify his statement.

Don't open your door unless the outside screen or storm is locked; keep the safety chain fastened. If necessary, you can talk through a locked door and check the stranger's I.D. through your peephole or by having him or her pass it under the door to you. Refuse to admit the person if there is any doubt in your mind. Not even the police have a right to enter your home without proper identification (which in that instance includes a warrant signed by a judge).

Sometimes your better nature may be put to severe tests. For example, a stranger comes to your door asking to use your phone because of an emergency, or to tell you someone in your family has been injured or killed in an accident. You can help a stranded motorist by making a call for him while he waits outside. The same applies for someone informing you of a mishap experienced by someone in your family. Keep them outside while you call hospitals or police to verify the facts.

USING CCTV

■ Closed-circuit television (CCTV) systems to monitor entryways, hallways or parking areas are within the budget of the average

You can set up your own CCTV system to monitor areas like entryways. This is how monitor would show person ringing your doorbell.

homeowner. In addition to offering the audio alarm of a bell or buzzer, CCTV offers the important dimension of sight. A complete home installation of a high-quality CCTV system can cost less than a new color TV set.

In its simplest form, a CCTV system is comprised of a television camera connected to a television monitor with a coaxial cable. The heart of the system is the camera. Some cameras have automatic light-compensating circuits that allow them to produce a usable picture from conditions ranging from dim lighting to bright sunshine. Such cameras operate for long periods without requiring any adjustment. The only component to wear out is the vidicon pickup tube which has a life expectancy of two years when the camera is operated 24 hours a day.

The TV monitor is similar in appearance to a regular TV set except that it has less internal circuitry. CCTV monitors are built so that you can add more than one monitor to the existing system, a practice called looping. An example of monitor looping would be to have TV Monitor No. 1 in the kitchen, Monitor No. 2 in the bedroom and Monitor No. 3 in some other room.

CCTV systems are available with a built-in intercom unit which allows the viewer to talk to the person ringing the doorbell. This

Components of CCTV system, including coaxial cable, built-in intercom unit (in cable), camera and monitor.

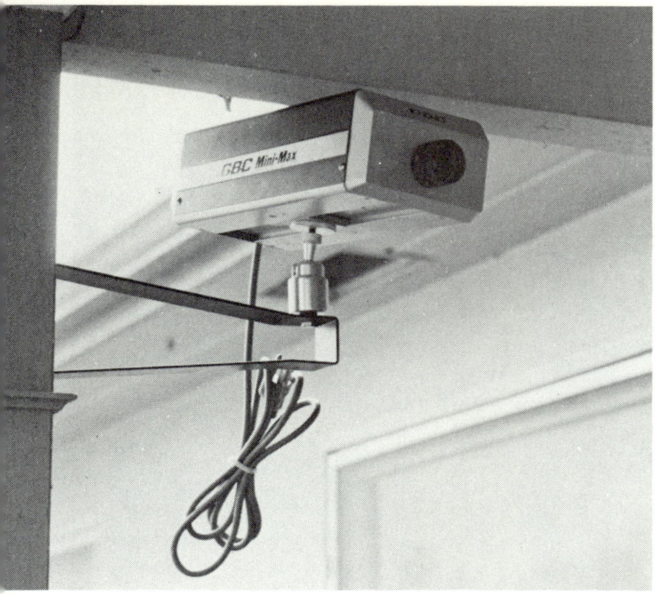

Camera, in place on camera mount, is aimed at view desired and adjusted later using monitor.

CCTV monitor installed in kitchen. Monitor should be positioned so it is viewed from 3′ to 15′ away.

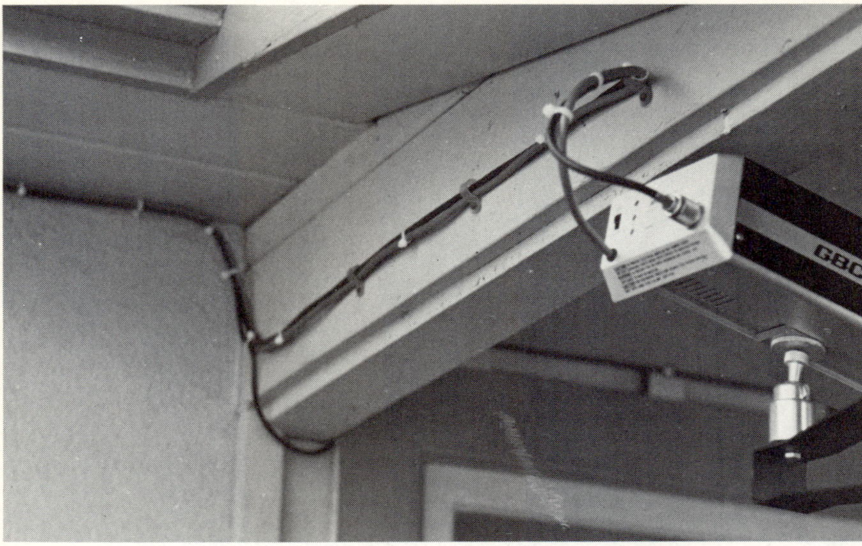

Cable is run from camera to monitor in most convenient way. Power, video and intercom audio cables can be run in one bundle.

arrangement gives an added benefit of turning away the overeager salesman without having to leave some important task in the home. You could place the camera to view the front door, install an intercom unit to replace the existing doorbell, and locate the TV monitor and matching intercom unit in the kitchen. Since just about every home is different in both arrangement and size, each installation will differ. However, the general installation steps outlined here will be similar.

1. Select the area to be viewed. Determine if lighting conditions will be adequate at night. The illumination from the existing porch light may do the trick. See if there is AC power near where the camera is to be located. If not, how far away is it? Some cameras have a variable voltage feature which allows you to use 28v current; this means you could place the camera up to 500′ from the closest AC outlet without the expense of having an electrician install a long run. Simply run up to 500′ of zip cord in the same bundle as the video coaxial cable and then use a standard 28v doorbell transformer at the AC outlet end.
2. After the area to be viewed is selected, install the camera

mount. This usually requires two or three screws or bolts. The camera mount is a friction device that uses a ball swivel to position a camera at many different angles. A hex-type adjusting screw is loosened and tightened for positioning.

3. Mount the camera and aim it toward the approximate field of view desired. *Note:* The camera vidicon tube is subject to "burn-in." This is a condition in which an image actually burns in on the faceplate of the vidicon if the camera is pointed at an area that has a very bright (hot) spot, such as a naked light bulb, for any length of time. After burn-in occurs, the original burned-in image will be seen on the monitor no matter where the camera is pointing. You can diffuse a light bulb with a shade or, in the case of a solid white area reflecting bright sunlight, you may have to paint the area another color. Never point a TV camera at direct sunlight.

   When activating the system, bring the monitor out to the vicinity of the camera so you can observe the picture while making setup adjustments. With coaxial cable connecting camera to monitor, apply power. Observe the picture while adjusting the camera mount to give the exact field of view desired. Next, tighten the friction-adjusting screw and carefully adjust the focus ring on the lens assembly of the camera until you get a crisp, clear picture. Next adjust both brightness and contrast controls.

4. Return the monitor to its permanent location. Some important considerations on monitor placement are these:

   ■ Check light level in the area where the monitor is to be located. Most monitors have enough brightness to permit operation in well-illuminated areas. However, it's best to keep the ambient light as low as possible to prevent the picture from having a washed-out look.

   ■ There is a possibility of an annoying reflection coming from the face of the monitor. Find another location. If this is not possible, change the location of the offending light. For comfortable viewing, the monitor should be located so the distance from the monitor to the viewer is from 3′ to 15′.

   ■ See if the monitor will have adequate ventilation for cooling. Locations near radiators or hot pipes or in enclosed niches should be avoided.

5. Route the video cable (and intercom audio cable, if used) taking the most convenient way between the camera and monitor. Power video and intercom audio cables can be run in one bundle from point A to point B.
6. Every camera has three basic adjustments. These are Target (T), Focus (F) and Beam (B). Rough handling in transportation, camera aging or different site conditions may make it necessary to readjust the camera for optimum picture quality.

   You can design your own CCTV with expansion in mind. Some expansion ideas are:

   ■ Adding more cameras to cover more locations and using only one monitor. This is accomplished by the use of a sequential switcher. Four or more cameras can be fed to one switcher and the scenes will automatically switch from one camera to another at a predetermined time period.

   ■ Adding a scanner. This allows the camera to sweep back and forth for a much wider field of view.

   ■ Adding an environmental or tamper-proof housing—necessary for inclement weather conditions.

POLICE PATROLS

■ Contrary to what you might believe, law-enforcement agencies urge homeowners to report any and all suspicious activity in their neighborhoods. If you observe out-of-the-ordinary activities or cars, don't hesitate to call the police or sheriff's department. If such activities happen frequently, you can ask for a police squad-check.

The theory behind most police patrols is that crime is discouraged when criminals believe that police on the scene will respond in time to arrest them immediately, and that random patrols may result in a police-suspect confrontation at any time.

Police modify their patrol patterns to give the most vulnerable targets the greatest protection. The best protection is a combination of repeated random patrols and a check of the premises. Officers checking out property on foot may try the doors, inspect ground-level windows and generally stay alert for clues to the presence of burglars—tape on a pane of glass, a crowbar lying on the ground, a screwdriver on a window sill, an unlocked door or perhaps a lookout car parked at a nearby corner.

Police departments, however, don't always have the personnel to perform much more than the most perfunctory building checks. Patrolmen "take a swing by" the addresses listed in their watch book, hoping to scare away would-be intruders. If you request that a squad check your home, you may receive only one or two extra visits a week. This is particularly true in areas where the demands on police time include ambulance service, minor-accident reporting and transporting the elderly and the indigent.

When you call for a patrol to check your home, ask about the squad-check techniques used by your local police. Ask the police how the squad is notified of your request. Is the officer required to log the times he visits your home? Do police supervisors take an interest in seeing that squads patrol neighborhoods? How often is the squad likely to check on your house? Will the officer leave the squad car?

PHONE SECURITY

■ One method a criminal can use to establish that your home is unoccupied is to make a phone call. If no one answers, the burglar can take the next step and ring the doorbell, just to stay on the safe side, or force entry immediately. A burglar also may call your number from a pay phone and leave for your home. If the phone is still ringing when he arrives, he knows chances are good it's unoccupied.

A simple way to foil burglars who case by phone is to arrange matters so that your phone is always answered. This doesn't have to be as expensive or involved as you might guess. One of the most economical phone services, available in many exchanges that have electronic switching, is something called call forwarding. With this system, you can instruct the phone company to transfer any phone calls from your home to any other phone that can be reached by dialing seven digits. It's like having your phone with you wherever you are, and the cost can be as little as a couple of dollars a month.

It works this way. You dial a two-digit code. The code signals the phone company's switching equipment to operate in the transfer mode. Then you dial the number that calls are to be forwarded to. Forwarding continues until you instruct the switcher to return to the normal mode by dialing another two-digit code. This system provides a high degree of flexibility, since all that is necessary is that someone at the forwarding number take the calls—you, a secretary, a housebound friend or relative.

An answering service can help you maintain the impression that someone is always home. It's particularly useful if you live alone or are unusually dependent on telephones for maintaining social and business contacts, and yet seldom remain in any one place long enough to make or get many calls. Seven-day-a-week, 24-hour service can cost less than $50 a month. Operators can be instructed to answer the phone in such a way that callers never know if you're actually at home or not.

An answering machine can help maintain a "telephone presence" in your home. It can be set up to imply that you are home but too busy to talk. Answering machines are relatively inexpensive—less than $100 for a basic playback unit. More sophisticated models that sell for a little over $100 allow you to collect your messages over the phone.

If you consider incoming phone calls a nuisance, could care less about offending callers and are worried about unexpected, uninvited or unauthorized calls, consider combining all three types of answering service. For example, you could use call forwarding for times when calls should be answered—when people might normally expect you to be available and have a problem that can't wait. You could use an answering service when polite, personalized message-taking is a must. And you could use a talking machine when expecting irritating, offensive or unwanted calls.

Be wary of repeated wrong numbers. If you receive an obscene phone call, hang up immediately. Try to show no reaction, and never reveal any information. Notify police and the telephone company of the calls. If necessary, get an unlisted phone number.

HIRING BABYSITTERS

■ Your home is more vulnerable when under the supervision of a babysitter. If a stranger knocks at the door, or if a fire or other emergency occurs, you should be reasonably sure you know how the sitter will respond. To avoid embarrassment, remorse or even tragedy, try to see that the conduct of a babysitter will be the same in your absence as it would be if you were present.

It helps to know the babysitter either personally or through investigation. If you don't know the sitter personally, try to get local references to check out. If the sitter is a minor, contact the parents. Get their approval, and check on the sitter's background. Have a

BABYSITTER'S GUIDE

EMERGENCY NUMBERS:

Fire Department ______________________

Police/Sheriff's Department ______________________

Doctor ______________________

ADDRESS HERE: ______________________

WILL BE AT: ______________________ PHONE ______________

WILL RETURN AT: ______________________

NEIGHBOR: ______________________ PHONE ______________

BEDTIME: ______________________

____

MEDICATIONS: ______________________

SPECIAL INSTRUCTIONS: ______________________

____

____

CALLS RECEIVED: ______________________

____

____

DO NOT OPEN THE DOOR TO ANYONE YOU DO NOT KNOW. IF YOU SEE OR HERE ANYTHING SUSPICIOUS, CALL THE POLICE. KEEP ALL OUTSIDE DOORS LOCKED.

Source: Anoka County (MN) Sheriff's Office

clear agreement on the terms of employment, including hours and rates.

Before you leave the sitter in charge, explain clearly what you expect him or her to do. Show the sitter that all doors and windows are locked. Make sure you write down emergency telephone numbers as indicated on the form shown here. Include where you or a responsible relative, neighbor or friend may be reached, and the numbers of the fire department, police or sheriff's department and your doctor. Put the list next to the phone and point it out.

Also instruct the sitter to either ignore the ringing of the doorbell and knocks at the door, or to take messages only through a locked door or window. Tell the sitter never to admit strangers, even those who claim to be your friends or on some kind of official business. If the visitor is insistent, have the sitter tell him to wait outside while a call is made to you or one of the other adults on the emergency list. It may be wise to summon a neighbor or a law-enforcement officer.

Tell the sitter how you want incoming telephone calls handled. The caller should be told you are "not able to come to the phone," never that you are away from home. Have the sitter take a message and write it down, or take the caller's number if an immediate call-back is desired. In the latter case, the sitter should relay the number to you without delay.

Introduce the sitter to the children, and let them get acquainted in your presence. Suggest how often to check the children, and advise the sitter of any unusual habits (sleepwalking, etc.) and of precautions to be taken.

If feedings are necessary, have the food ready and show the sitter where it's located. Also lay out snacks for the sitter.

Show the sitter where all facilities are located, and explain the operation of any appliances that may be used, such as the television. This minimizes the chances of inadvertent harm to your property or to the sitter. Explain that you do not allow guests. A possible exception may be one friend of the same sex.

Ask the sitter for a report on any unusual incidents during your absence. If he or she has a deadline or if you have said you will be home at a certain time, be punctual. If there is a delay, call the sitter and explain it.

All minor babysitters should be transported to their homes. This is recommended for older sitters as well, if feasible, but the latter should at least be delivered to the closest line of public transportation. If the sitter must wait alone at an isolated spot, stay on hand until transportation arrives.

ON-THE-ROAD PROTECTION

- When traveling, keep valuables on your person, not in your pocketbook.Try to use credit cards and traveler's checks instead of cash.

This electronic intruder alarm can be taken with you to protect windows and doors, passageways, room areas, cars or other vehicles. Cord, anchored by self-adhesive pad, attaches to any article, or stretches across any area and triggers alarm siren if there is any change in its tension.

This unit is portable, and electronically protects you against intrusion and fire either at home or in rented rooms. It costs less than $15, complete with batteries.

This unit can be used at home or taken on the road. About the size of a cigarette pack, it operates on two 9v batteries to emit 106-decibel sweeping siren at the slightest movement. You adjust sensitivity control to desired level.

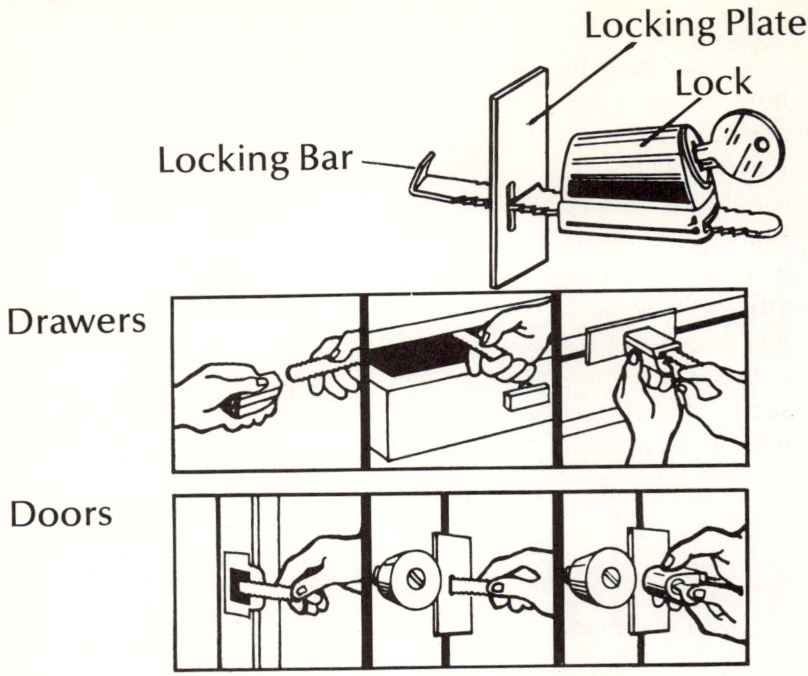

ıis all-purpose travel lock provides key control for hotel and motel doors and Jrawers, and for other security uses. Key unlocks unit to slide out locking bar. After drawer or door is opened, locking bar is hooked into rectangular door-jamb hole or onto rigid member above inside drawer. Drawer or door is closed, and locking plate is slid onto bar horizontally or vertically as desired. Lock is slid onto locking bar tight against locking plate.

When shopping, don't leave your purse or wallet in your basket or on a counter. At night, travel in well-lit areas, preferably with a companion. Never pick up hitchhikers or hitchhike yourself.

Don't leave your car at airport parking lots for long periods while you're away. Besides the danger of vandalism or theft, there is the possibility of thieves tracing the license plate number back to your house. When using your own or rented cars, park near streetlights at night and avoid ill-lit parking places. Make sure no one is hiding in the backseat before you enter the car. Keep windows closed and doors locked while you're in the car. Store valuables in the trunk and not on the car seat. When you expect to return to your own home after dark, leave a light on in the garage.

Don't leave keys or I.D. cards in your car. Keep your house keys and car keys on separate chains. Never put your address on key chains.

If you check into hotel or motel rooms, take a look around to see how secure your room is. Most hotel or motel managements will check valuables, though their liability will be within specified limits. Keep your doors locked at all times, including doors to connecting rooms. A variety of locks are available for use in rented rooms. Some of them can be used to make a "safe" out of the top drawer of a dresser to store items you don't want to check. They can help you enjoy greater security against burglars or dishonest hotel employees who may have keys to the rooms.

Besides using locks, you can do some improvising to boost the security of your room. For example, a drawer hung on the doorknob with items perched on it can serve as a makeshift alarm.

APPENDIX

Below is a partial listing of companies that offer equipment and services that can help increase home security.

ALARMS, BURGLAR

ADT
One World Trade Center
92nd Floor
New York, N.Y. 10048

Andover Corp.
Shetland Industrial Park
Haverhill St.
Andover, Mass. 01801

Blaine Window Hardware
McDade Rd., Rt. 4
Hagerstown, Md. 21740

Fyrnetics
920 Davis Rd.
Elgin, Ill. 60120

G & G Enterprises
P. O. Box 146
Davisburg, Mich. 48019

J. T. Hines Associates
23 Haddonfield Dr.
Parsippany, N.J. 07054

Hoffman Co., Inc.
427 Pulaski Rd.
Greenlawn, N.Y. 11740

Holes-Webway Co.
Webway Park
St. Cloud, Minn. 56301

Honeywell Protection
1107 Peters St.
Dallas, Tex. 75215

Ideal Security Hardware
215 E. 9th St.
St. Paul, Minn. 55107

JS & A National Sales
One JS & A Plaza
Northbrook, Ill. 60062

Master Lock Co.
2600 N. 32nd St.
Milwaukee, Wis. 53210

NuTone
Div. Scovill
Madison and Red Bank Rds.
Cincinnati, Ohio 45227

Radio Shack
Tandy Corp.
Fort Worth, Tex. 76107

S. Parker Hardware Mfg. Co.
27 Ludlow St.
New York, N.Y. 10002

Sears
Sears Tower
Chicago, Ill. 60684

Speedex Electronics
400 S. Wyman
Rockford, Ill. 61109

Suburban Electronics
1250 W. Dorothy Lane
Dayton, Ohio 45409

SVS Surveillance Systems
2315 E. 7th Ave.
Denver, Colo. 80206

Thomas Industries
207 E. Broadway
Louisville, Ky. 40202

3M
Alarm Services
500 11th Ave. S.
Minneapolis, Minn. 55415

Trine Mfg.
1430 Ferris Place
Bronx, N.Y. 10461

Ultra Electronics
10315 Woodley Ave.
Granada Hills, Calif. 91344

Waldom Electronics
4625 W. 53rd St.
Chicago, Ill. 60632

John Weil Co.
1770 Lexington Ave.
New York, N.Y. 10024

ALARMS, GAS DETECTOR

Craftor, Inc.
1237 Central Ave.
Albany, N.Y. 12205

McGraw-Edison
1801 N. Stadium Blvd.
Columbia, Mo. 65201

Pittway Corp.
780 McClure Ave.
Aurora, Ill. 60507

John Weil Co.
1770 Lexington Ave.
New York, N.Y. 10024

ALARMS, PERSONAL

Safety Guard
10568 Magnolia St.
Suite 110
Anaheim, Calif. 92804

Westcoast Enterprises
17158 Buttonwood St.
Suite F16
Fountain Valley, Calif. 92708

ALARMS, POWER FAILURE

Waldom Electronics
4301 W. 69th St.
Chicago, Ill. 60629

ALARMS, SMOKE DETECTOR

American House
8 Sandy St.
East Northport, N.Y. 11731

Eagle Electric
45–31 Court Square
Long Island City, N.Y. 11101

Fyrnetics
920 Davis Rd.
Elgin, Ill. 60120

General Electric Co.
600 Third Ave.
38th Floor
New York, N.Y. 10016

Golin Communications
500 N. Michigan Ave.
Chicago, Ill. 60611

H & V Enterprises
P.O. Box 8139
Salt Lake City, Utah 84108

J. T. Hines Associates
23 Haddonfield Dr.
Parsippany, N.J. 07054

Hoffman Co., Inc.
427 Pulaski Rd.
Greenlawn, N.Y. 11740

Holes-Webway Co.
Webway Park
St. Cloud, Minn. 56301

Honeywell Residential Div.
Honeywell Plaza
Minneapolis, Minn. 55408

Kwikset Sales and Service
516 E. Santa Ana St.
Anaheim, Calif. 92803

Master Lock
2600 N. 32nd St.
Milwaukee, Wis. 53210

NuTone
Div. Scovill
Madison and Red Bank Rds.
Cincinnati, Ohio 45227

Perfect Line Mfg. Corp.
80 E. Gates Ave.
Lindenhurst, N.Y. 11757

Sylvania
General Telephone
& Electronics
One Stamford Forum
Stamford, Conn. 06904

Teledyne Water Pik, Inc.
1730 E. Prospect St.
Fort Collins, Colo. 80521

Thomas Industries
207 E. Broadway
Louisville, Ky. 40202

Trine Mfg.
1430 Ferris Place
Bronx, N.Y. 10461

Weslock
TRE Corp.
13344 S. Main St.
Los Angeles, Calif. 90061

Westel Corp.
111 N. Central Ave.
Hartsdale, N.Y. 10530

ALARMS, WEATHER

Realistic
1301 W. Armitage
Melrose Park, Ill. 60160

BICYCLE SECURITY

Bike Security Systems
177 Tosca Dr.
Stoughton, Mass. 02072

CAR SECURITY

Identicar International
217 W. Central St.
Natick, Mass. 01760

Oakridge Industries
Box 21560
Cleveland, Ohio 44121

Page Alert Systems
23840 Madison St.
Torrance, Calif. 90505

Phone Control Systems
92 Marcus Ave.
New Hyde Park, N.Y. 11040

The Pine Cone
7485 Monterey St.
Box 1378
Gilroy, Calif. 95020

W. Roche Co.
3816 N. Oak Grove N522
Midwest City, Okla. 73110

Ronson House Gard-A-Car
2711 E. 27th St.
Kansas City, Mo. 64127

DEADBOLTS

Arrow Lock Corp.
4900 Glenwood Rd.
Brooklyn, N.Y. 11234

Donner Mfg. Co.
12860 Bradley Ave.
Sylmar, Calif. 91342

Eaton Corp.
Yale Marketing Dept.
P.O. Box 25288
Charlotte, N.C. 28212

Ideal Security Hardware
215 E. 9th St.
St. Paul, Minn. 55107

ILCO/Unican
400 Fawn Dr.
Rocky Mount, N.C. 27801

National Lock Co.
Sikeston, Mo. 53801

S. Parker Hardware Mfg. Co.
27 Ludlow St.
New York, N.Y. 10002

Weiser Lock
4100 Ardmore Ave.
Southgate, Calif. 90280

Weslock
TRE Corp.
13344 S. Main St.
Los Angeles, Calif. 90061

DOOR CHAINS

American Tack & Hardware
25 Robert Pitt Dr.
Monsey, N.Y. 10952

Amerock Corp.
4000 Auburn St.
Rockford, Ill. 61101

Better Way Products
21330 Center Ridge Rd.
Rocky River, Ohio 44116

Eaton Corp.
Yale Marketing Dept.
P.O. Box 25288
Charlotte, N.C. 28212

Holmes-Hally Industries
7460 Bandini Blvd.
Los Angeles, Calif. 90040

Ideal Security Hardware
215 E. 9th St.
St. Paul, Minn. 55107

ILCO/Unican
400 Fawn Dr.
Rocky Mount, N.C. 27801

Kwikset Sales and Service
516 E. Santa Ana St.
Anaheim, Calif. 92803

St. Croix Corp.
9909 South Shore Dr.
Minneapolis, Minn. 55441

Stanley Hardware
195 Lake St.
New Britain, Conn. 06050

Arthur P. Steele Corp.
30 Cummings Pk.
Woburn, Mass. 01801

Weil Service Products
2434 W. Fletcher St.
Chicago, Ill. 60618

Weiser Lock
4100 Ardmore Ave.
Southgate, Calif. 90280

Wright Products
107 W. Coleman
Rice Lake, Wis. 54868

DOOR HARDWARE

Belwith International
7600 Industry Ave.
Pico Rivera, Calif. 93550

Blaine Window Hardware
McDade Rd., Rt. 4
Hagerstown, Md. 21740

Ideal Security Hardware
215 E. 9th St.
St. Paul, Minn. 55107

Lawrence Brothers
Sterling, Ill. 61081

National Mfg. Co.
P.O. Box 577
Sterling, Ill. 61081

P.T.I.-Dilco
13401 S. Main St.
Los Angeles, Calif. 90061

Sentry Door Lock Guards, Inc.
114 S.W. 3rd Ave.
Dania, Fla. 33004

DOOR VIEWERS

Amerock Corp.
4000 Auburn St.
Rockford, Ill. 61101

Baker Security Ltd.
1 W. Forest Ave.
Englewood, N.J. 07631

NuTone
Div. Scovill
Madison and Red Bank Rds.
Cincinnati, Ohio 45227

S. Parker Hardware Mfg. Co.
27 Ludlow St.
New York, N.Y. 10002

Stanley Hardware
195 Lake St.
New Britain, Conn. 06050

Weiser Lock
4100 Ardmore Ave.
Southgate, Calif. 90280

FIRE ESCAPE LADDERS

American LaFrance
P.O. Box 6159
Charlottesville, Va. 22906

Daverson Enterprises
21 Saw Mill River Rd.
Yonkers, N.Y. 10701

Rival Mfg. Co.
36th and Bennington
Kansas City, Mo. 64129

FIRE EXTINGUISHERS

Amerex Corp.
P.O. Box 81
Trussville, Ala. 35173

American LaFrance
P.O. Box 6159
Charlottesville, Va. 22906

Ansul Co.
Marinette, Wis. 54143

Bernzomatic Corp.
Rochester, N.Y. 14613

Buckeye Fire Equipment Co.
102 Industrial Dr.
Kings Mtn., N.C. 28086

Gillette
Prudential Tower Bldg.
Boston, Mass. 02199

Walter Kidde & Co.
675 Main St.
Belleville, N.J. 07109

Pem All Corp.
39A Myrtle St.
Cranford, N.J. 07016

GARAGE DOOR OPENERS

Alliance Mfg. Co.
22790 Lake Park Blvd.
Alliance, Ohio 44601

Blaine Window Hardware
McDade Rd., Rt. 4
Hagerstown, Md. 21740

Chamberlain Mfg. Co.
845 Larch Ave.
Elmhurst, Ill. 60126

Franz Mfg. Co.
301 W. 3rd St.
Sterling, Ill. 61081

Miami-Carey
203 Garver Rd.
Monroe, Ohio 45050

NuTone
Div. Scovill
Madison and Red Banks Rds.
Cincinnati, Ohio 45227

Stanley Hardware
195 Lake St.
New Britain, Conn. 06050

INSURANCE COMPANIES

(Partial listing of companies known to offer discounts on homeowners insurance with approved fire and burglar protection. Note: The companies offering discounts, and the specific discounts offered can change over time. It's best to check with your agent in all cases.)

Aetna Life and Casualty
151 Farmington Ave.
Hartford, Conn. 06115

American States Ins. Co.
P.O. Box 1636
500 N. Meridian
Indianapolis, Ind. 46207

Chubb Corp. Group
100 Williams St.
New York, N.Y. 10038

CNA Ins. Group
CNA Plaza
Chicago, Ill. 60685

Commercial Union Ins. Co.
1 Beacon St.
Boston, Mass. 02181

Continental Ins. Group
360 W. Jackson Blvd.
Chicago, Ill. 60606

Crum & Forster Ins. Co.
P.O. Box 2387
Morristown, N.J. 07960

Fireman's Fund
Lock Box 3395
San Francisco, Calif. 94119

Government Employees Ins. Co.
3520 Lake
Wilmette, Ill. 60091

Great American Ins. Cos.
580 Walnut St.
P.O. Box 2575
Cincinnati, Ohio 45201

Harleysville Mutual
355 Maple Ave.
Harleysville, Pa. 19438

Home Ins. Cos.
59 Maiden Lane
New York, N.Y. 10038

INA Corp.
P.O. Box 7728
Philadelphia, Pa. 19101

Kemper Ins. Cos.
Central Div.
Long Grove, Ill. 60049

Ohio Casualty Group
Hamilton, Ohio 45025

Royal-Globe Ins. Cos.
150 Williams St.
New York, N.Y. 10038

St. Paul Group
385 Washington St.
St. Paul, Minn. 55102

State Farm Group
1 State Farm Plaza
Bloomington, Ill. 61701

Transamerica Ins. Group
1150 S. Olive St.
Los Angeles, Calif. 90015

Travelers Group
1 Tower Square
Hartford, Conn. 06115

USAA Group
9800 Fredericksburg Rd.
San Antonio, Tex. 78288

U.S. Fidelity & Guaranty Group
100 Light St.
P.O. Box 1138
Baltimore, Md. 21203

Utica National Group
P.O. Box 851
Utica, N.Y. 13503

Zurich-American Ins. Cos.
111 W. Jackson Blvd.
Chicago, Ill. 60604

KEYS AND ACCESSORIES

Cole National Corp.
5777 Grant Ave.
Cleveland, Ohio 44105

Newell-Bulldog Co.
916 S. Arcade
Freeport, Ill. 61032

Schlage Lock Co.
P.O. Box 3324
San Francisco, Calif. 94119

LIGHTNING PROTECTION

Carl Bajohr Co., Inc.
801 Commercial Rd.
P.O. Box 2127
Jonesboro, Ark. 72401

General Electric
Circuit Protection Devices
Plainville, Conn. 06062

Independent Protection Co.
1603–09 S. Main St.
Goshen, Ind. 46526

Lightning Protection Inst.
48 N. Ayer St.
Harvard, Ill. 60033

Thompson Lightning Protection
901 Sibley Hwy.
St. Paul, Minn. 55118

West Dodd Lightning Corp.
116 W. Lafayette St.
Goshen, Ind. 46526

LOCK INSTALLING EQUIPMENT

Security Supply Service
285 Newtonville Ave.
Newtonville, Mass. 02160

LOCK SETS

Amerock Corp.
4000 Auburn St.
Rockford, Ill. 61101

Arrow Lock Co.
4900 Glenwood Rd.
Brooklyn, N.Y. 11234

Brooks National Hardware
87–46 123rd St.
Richmond Hills, N.Y. 11418

Citadel
177 Tosca Dr.
Stoughton, Mass. 02072

Dexter Lock
1601 Madison S.E.
Grand Rapids, Mich. 49507

Donner Mfg.
12860 Bradley Ave.
Sylmar, Calif. 91342

Eaton Corp.
Yale Marketing Dept.
P.O. Box 25288
Charlotte, N.C. 28212

Electronic Security System
P.O. Box 61403
Sunnyvale, Calif. 94088

Globemaster
9714 Old Katy Rd.
Houston, Tex. 77055

Howard Hardware Products
P.O. Box 589
Bloomfield, N.J. 07003

Ideal Security Hardware
215 E. 9th St.
St. Paul, Minn. 55107

ILCO/Unican
400 Fawn Dr.
Rocky Mount, N.C. 27801

Kwikset Sales and Service
516 E. Santa Ana St.
Anaheim, Calif. 92803

Loxem Mfg. Corp.
P.O. Box 190
1201 Exchange Dr.
Richardson, Tex. 75080

National Lock Co.
Sikeston, Mo. 53801

New England Lock
and Hardware
South Norwalk, Conn. 06856

Oakridge Industries
Box 21560
Cleveland, Ohio 44121

S. Parker Hardware Mfg. Co.
27 Ludlow St.
New York, N.Y. 10002

Parker Metal Corp.
85 Prescott St.
Worcester, Mass. 01605

Pease
7100 Dixie Hwy.
Fairfield, Ohio 45023

Schlage Lock Co.
P.O. Box 3324
San Francisco, Calif. 94119

Sentry Door Lock Guards, Inc.
114 S.W. 3rd Ave.
Dania, Fla. 33004

Arthur P. Steele Corp.
30 Cummings Pk.
Woburn, Mass. 01801

Weiser Lock
4100 Ardmore Ave.
Southgate, Calif. 90280

Weslock
TRE Corp.
13344 S. Main St.
Los Angeles, Calif. 90061

Wright Products
107 W. Coleman
Rice Lake, Wis. 54868

PADLOCKS

Benton Co.
114 Carrier St.
Liberty, N.Y. 12754

Brooks National Hardware
87–46 123rd St.
Richmond, N.Y. 11418

Campbell Chain Co.
3990 E. Market St.
York, Pa. 17402

Donner Mfg. Co.
12860 Bradley Ave.
Sylmar, Calif. 91342

Eaton Corp.
Yale Marketing Dept.
P.O. Box 25288
Charlotte, N.C. 28212

Howard Hardware Products
P.O. Box 589
Bloomfield, N.J. 07003

ILCO/Unican
400 Fawn Dr.
Rocky Mount, N.C. 27801

Lawson, Reed & Co.
High Meadow Rd.
Guilford, Conn. 06437

Loxem Mfg. Corp.
P.O. Box 190
1201 Exchange Dr.
Richardson, Tex. 75080

Master Lock Co.
2600 N. 32nd St.
Milwaukee, Wis. 53210

National Mfg. Co.
P.O. Box 577
Sterling, Ill. 61081

S. Parker Hardware Mfg. Co.
27 Ludlow St.
New York, N.Y. 10002

Arthur P. Steele Corp.
30 Cummings Pk.
Woburn, Mass. 01801

John W. Tulppo
P.O. Box 44
Wakefield, Mich. 49968

Weil Service Products
2434 W. Fletcher St.
Chicago, Ill. 60618

Weiser Lock
4100 Ardmore Ave.
South Gate, Calif. 90280

Wilbert-Fischer Co.
8608 San Carlos Ave.
South Gate, Calif. 90280

World Wide Trade
80 School St.
Watertown, Mass. 02172

SECURITY BOXES AND SAFES

John D. Brush & Co.
900 Linden Ave.
Rochester, N.Y. 14625

Deerfield Lock Co.
Deerfield, Ill. 60015

Lee Metal Products
Littletown, Pa. 17340

Miles Osborn
P.O. Box 15210
Santa Ana, Calif. 92705

The Seasons Four
2510 S. Brentwood Blvd.
Suite 301
Brentwood, Mo. 63144

SVS Surveillance
2315 E. 7th Ave.
Denver, Colo. 80206

SECURITY CABLES AND CHAINS

Campbell Chain Co.
3990 E. Market St.
York, Pa. 17402

ILCO/Unican
400 Fawn Dr.
Rocky Mount, N.C. 27801

Master Lock Co.
2600 N. 32nd St.
Milwaukee, Wis. 53210

S. Parker Hardware Mfg. Co.
27 Ludlow St.
New York, N.Y. 10002

Stanley Hardware
195 Lake St.
New Britain, Conn. 06050

Arthur P. Steele Corp.
30 Cummings Pk.
Woburn, Mass. 01801

SECURITY DOORS

Grisham Corp.
1811 Bartlett Rd.
Memphis, Tenn. 38134

Stanley Door Systems
2400 E. Lincoln
Birmingham, Mich. 48012

Steelcraft
9017 Blue Ash Rd.
Cincinnati, Ohio 45242

SECURITY GLASS

Plaskolite
1770 Joyce Ave.
Columbus, Ohio 43219

Rohm & Haas
Commercial Plastic Corp.
1642 Woodhaven Dr.
Cornwell Hghts., Pa. 19020

Transparent Glass Co.
1959 S. LaCienega Blvd.
Los Angeles, Calif. 90034

SECURITY HARDWARE

Ajax Hardware
825 S. Ajax Ave.
City of Industry, Calif. 91749

American Tack & Hardware
25 Robert Pitt Dr.
Monsey, N.Y. 10952

Amerock Corp.
4000 Auburn St.
Rockford, Ill. 61101

Belwith International
7600 Industry Ave.
Pico Rivera, Calif. 93550

Blaine Window Hardware
McDade Rd., Rt. 4
Hagerstown, Md. 21740

Brainerd Mfg. Corp.
115 N. Washington St.
East Rochester, N.Y. 14445

R. R. Brooks Co.
7326 Jefferson St.
Paramount, Calif. 90723

Dexter Lock
1601 Madison S.E.
Grand Rapids, Mich. 49507

Donner Mfg.
12860 Bradley Ave.
Sylmar, Calif. 91342

Eaton Corp.
Yale Marketing Dept.
P.O. Box 25288
Charlotte, N.C. 28212

Ideal Security Hardware
215 E. 9th St.
St. Paul, Minn. 55107

ILCO/Unican
400 Fawn Dr.
Rocky Mount, N.C. 27801

KinKead Industries
Div. United States Gypsum
5860 N. Pulaski Rd.
Chicago, Ill. 60646

Kwikset Sales and Service
516 E. Santa Ana St.
Anaheim, Calif. 92803

Lawrence Brothers
Sterling, Ill. 61081

Leigh Products
411 64th St.
Coopersville, Mich. 49404

Loxem Mfg. Corp.
P.O. Box 190
1201 Exchange Dr.
Richardson, Tex. 75080

Master Lock Co.
2600 N. 32nd St.
Milwaukee, Wis. 53210

National Mfg. Co.
P.O. Box 577
Sterling, Ill. 61081

S. Parker Hardware Mfg. Co.
27 Ludlow St.
New York, N.Y. 10002

Parker Metal Corp.
85 Prescott St.
Worcester, Mass. 01605

Philstone Nail Corp.
57 Pine St.
Canton, Mass. 02021

Plaskolite
1770 Joyce Ave.
Columbus, Ohio 43219

P.T.I.-Dilco
13401 S. Main St.
Los Angeles, Calif. 90061

Schlage Lock Co.
P.O. Box 3324
San Francisco, Calif. 94119

Sentry Door Lock Guards, Inc.
114 S.W. 3rd Ave.
Dania, Fla. 33004

Stanley Hardware
195 Lake St.
New Britain, Conn. 06050

Weiser Lock
Div. Norris Ind.
4100 Ardmore Ave.
Southgate, Calif. 90280

Weslock
TRE Corp.
13344 S. Main St.
Los Angeles, Calif. 90061

Wessel Hardware Corp.
D St. and Erie Ave.
Philadelphia, Pa. 19134

Wright Products
107 W. Coleman
Rice Lake, Wis. 54868

SECURITY LIGHTING

Duro-Lite Lamps, Inc.
17–10 Willow St.
Fair Lawn, N.J. 07410

Edison Lighting
McGraw-Edison Co.
400 Busse Rd.
Elk Grove, Ill. 60007

General Electric Co.
600 Third Ave.
38th Floor
New York, N.Y. 10016

ITT Lighting
P.O. Box 30207
Memphis, Tenn. 38130

Little Giant Pump Co.
3810 N. Tulsa
Oklahoma City, Okla. 73312

Perfect-Lite Mfg. Corp.
80 E. Gates Ave.
Lindenhurst, N.Y. 11757

Rival Mfg. Co.
36th and Bennington
Kansas City, Mo. 64129

Thomas Industries
Residential Lighting Div.
207 E. Broadway
Louisville, Ky. 40202

SECURITY MARKING EQUIPMENT

Electric Engravers

Dremel Mfg. Co.
4915 21st St.
Racine, Wis. 53406

Burgess Vibrocrafters
Grayslake, Ill. 60030

Rockwell International
3171 Directors Row
Memphis, Tenn. 38131

Wen Products
5810 Northwest Hwy.
Chicago, Ill. 60631

Invisible-Ink Pens

Sanford Corp.
2740 Washington Blvd.
Bellwood, Ill. 60104

Scribers

Brookstone Co.
122 Vose Farm Rd.
Peterborough, N.H. 03458

Hart Systems
P.O. Box 49720
Los Angeles, Calif. 90049

TELEPHONE EQUIPMENT

Cedar Hill Service
Foristell, Mo. 63348

NuTone
Div. Scovill
Madison and Red Bank Rds.
Cincinnati, Ohio 45227

TIMERS

Eagle Electric Mfg. Co.
45–31 Court Square
Long Island City, N.Y. 11101

General Electric Co.
600 Third Ave.
38th Floor
New York, N.Y. 10016

NuTone
Div. Scovill
Madison and Red Bank Rds.
Cincinnati, Ohio 45227

Speedex Electronics
400 S. Wyman
Rockford, Ill. 61109

WINDOW HARDWARE

Amerock Corp.
4000 Auburn St.
Rockford, Ill. 61101

Blaine Window Hardware
McDade Rd., Rt. 4
Hagerstown, Md. 21740

R. R. Brooks Co.
7326 Jefferson St.
Paramount, Calif. 90723

Eaton Corp.
Yale Marketing Dept.
P.O. Box 25288
Charlotte, N.C. 28212

ILCO/Unican
400 Fawn Dr.
Rocky Mount, N.C. 27801

Lawrence Brothers
Sterling, Ill. 61081

Leslie-Locke
2872 W. Market St.
Akron, Ohio 44313

Season-all Industries
Indiana, Pa. 15701

Security Show Shelf
P.O. Box 14782
Austin, Tex. 78761

Soss Mfg. Co.
P.O. Box 8200
Detroit, Mich. 48213

Stanley Hardware
195 Lake St.
New Britain, Conn. 06050

Superior Security Iron, Inc.
6301 St. Louis Ave.
St. Louis, Mo. 63121

ADDITIONAL SECURITY INFORMATION

Crime Prevention

U.S. Small Business Admin.
Washington, D.C. 20416

Fire Protection

National Fire Protection
Association
470 Atlantic Ave.
Boston, Mass. 02210

Smoke Detector Information

National Bureau of Standards
Washington, D.C. 20234

INDEX

A

Acrylic windows, 59–63
Air conditioners, window, 58
Alarm(s)
- bells and horns, 150, 151, 153
- burglar, 14, 26, 147
- gas, 98
- sensors, 141, 142–143, 147, 149–150, 151, 152
- severe storm, 101
- smoke, 97
- types of, 144

Alarm system(s), 141–165
- monitoring, 145
- parts of, 141–143
- planning guide, 147
- wiring diagrams, 148, 155

Alternators, 124
Answering machine, 190
Answering service, 190
Antenna lightning discharge units, 132
Appliance failure monitors, 102
Attack dogs, 92–95
Automatic telephone dialer, 144
Automobile antitheft devices, 168–176
Auto theft, 166–168, 176–177

B

Babysitters, 190–192
Basement windows, 58
Beveled bolts, 43
Beveled-ring cylinder lock guard, 50
Black light, 71, 74
Black market, 12
Blackout protection, 124–132
Burglar profile, 22–25
Burglary
- protection, 27–28
- vulnerability to, 21–26, 30–34, 36–37

C

Call forwarding, 189, 190
Cam-action catch lock, 54
Casement window key lock, 55
Central-station telephone system, 144
Chain ladders, 13, 14, 121
"Charley-Bar," 55–56
Circuit-breaker GFI, 104–105
Closed-circuit TV systems, 183–188
Combination locks, 51
Control box, alarm, 147, 148, 152
Control systems, electric, 77–78
Costs, security equipment, 13–14
Cylindrical locks, 40, 41, 50–51

D

Deadbolt locks, 39, 41, 42, 49–50
Detectors. *See* specific types.
Direct-connect telephone system, 144
Disaster
- insurance, 17, 19
- preparation, 137–139
- recovery, 140

Dogs
- attack, 92–95
- guard, 26, 88–95

Door(s)
- alarms, 153
- gate, 30
- locks, 13, 14, 28–30, 35–52
- security, 35–39

Double cylinder deadbolt, 49

Double-hung windows, 28, 54
Downlighting, 87
Driving protection, 177–178
Dwelling insurance, 16–17

E

Emergency generators, 124
Emergency lighting, 131–132
Engravers, electric, 69, 74
Escape ladders, 13, 14, 121
Escutcheon plate, 50–51
Exterior lighting, 26, 78–87

F

Fire
- action plan, 119–121
- causes of, 108
- checklists, 108–109, 123
- codes, 97
- defense systems, 108–123, 147
- department home survey, 97
- escape equipment, 13, 14, 121
- extinguishers, 13, 14, 113–119
- insurance, 17, 18
- prevention, 109
- protection equipment, 13, 14, 108, 109–119, 122
- safes, 13, 14, 122
- statistics, 97, 108

Firearms, 182
First aid, 140
Floodlights, 78, 79, 81, 82–83
Floods, 139, 140
Fluorescent lights, 83
Folding ladders, 13, 14, 121

G

Garage door openers, 179–180
Garage security, 178–180
Gas detectors, 13, 14, 96, 98–100
Gas leaks, 98–99
Gates, door and window, 30, 54
Generators, emergency, 124
Glass blocks, installing, 63–64
Glass substitutes, window, 59–63
Ground fault interrupters, 102–107
Ground-lighting units, 81–83
Guard dogs, 26, 88–95
Gun accidents, 182

H

Hardwired alarms, 141, 154–165
Heat detectors, 147
Hinges, 39
Homeowners insurance, 14–20
Home-security measures, 26, 147
Home survey, 12

I

Identicar, 175–176
Identification, property, 26, 32, 34, 68–75
Infrared photoelectric sensors, 143, 147, 149
Insurance
- agents, 16
- companies, 15
- homeowners, 14–20
- premium discounts, 14, 20
- renters, 14

Intercoms, 182
Interior lighting, 76–78
Inventory sheets, 72–74
Invisible marking ink, 71, 74–75
Ionization smoke detectors, 98, 109

J

Jalousie doors, 38
Jalousie windows, 58
Jimmy-proof lock, 42, 44

K

Kennels, 92

Key-in-knob locks, 39–43
  replacing, 45–48
Keys, 51, 52

L

Ladders, escape, 13, 14, 121
Laminated glass, 38
Latches, 41
Light bulbs, 84
Lighting
  emergency, 131–132
  entranceways, 78
  exterior, 26, 78–87
  garages and parking areas, 83
  interior, 76–78
  low-voltage, 13, 84–87
  patios, 83
  pools, 83
  sources, 76
  steps, paths and walks, 80
  timers, 13, 33, 76–78
Lightning protection, 124, 132–136
Lightning rods, 132
Lights
  floodlights, 78, 79, 81, 82–83
  fluorescent, 83
  ground units, 81–83
  mercury lamps, 13, 78, 83
  mushroom, 79, 85, 87
  recessed, 78
  spotlights, 84, 85
  wall-mounted, 78
Line-carrier alarms, 141
Local alarms, 144
Lock(s)
  door, 13, 14, 28–30, 35–52
  hasps, 51
  quality, 50
  window, 13, 14, 28–30, 53, 54–58

M

Magnetic sensors, 147, 149
Match Key locks, 52
Mercury lamps, 13, 78, 83
Metal straps, window, 58
Monitor looping, 184
Mortise locks, 40, 43–44
Motion detectors, 143, 147, 149
Multipurpose fire extinguishers, 115, 116
Mushroom lights, 79, 85, 87

N

Natural disasters, 124, 136–140
Neighborhood crime watch, 75

O

Obscene phone calls, 190
Operation Identification, 68–74, 75

P

Padlocks, 51
Panic button alarms, 165
PAR floodlights, 78, 79, 81, 83
Patio doors, 38, 55, 57
Peepholes, 30, 38
Perils, insurance coverage of, 17, 19
Perimeter protection, 146, 147
Personal protection, 181–182
Photoelectric eyes, 84
Photoelectronic smoke detectors, 98, 109
Pin tumblers, 50
Plexiglass windows, 61–63
Plumbing, testing, 140
Police patrols, 188–189
Portable GFI, 106–107
Portable power plants, 124–131
Power failure detectors, 96, 102
Pressure mats, 143, 147, 150
Push buttons, emergency, 147

R

Recessed lighting, 78

Recreational vehicle theft, 178
Reflective light, 87
Remote alarms, 144, 147
Renters insurance, 14
Rim locks, 40, 44–49

S

Safes, 29, 31
  fire, 13, 14, 122
Sash locks, 54
Scribers, 75
Secondary service arresters, 132
Security doors, 35–39
Sensors, 141, 142–143, 147, 149–150, 151, 152
Shelters, storm, 137, 138, 139
Shunt switch, 153
Shutters, 65–67
Single cylinder deadbolt, 49
Sliding door bolts, 39
Sliding glass windows, 55–58
Smoke detectors, 13, 14, 96–98, 109–113, 147, 157
Spinner ring locks, 50
Spotlights, 84, 85
Square deadbolt, 49
Steering wheel locks, 170
Storm detectors, 13, 14, 100–101
Storm protection, 136–139
Strangers, dealing with, 182–183
Summer home, securing, 65
Surface locks, 39
Switch sensor, 143

T

Telephone dialer, 144, 147, 153
Telephone security, 189–190
Temperature monitor alarms, 102
Tempered glass, 59
Timers, lighting, 13, 33, 76–78
Tornado
  alarm, 101

Tornado (*cont.*)
  protection, 139
  statistics, 100, 136
Travel security, 189–190
Tree protection, 133–134
Tubular lock, 41
TV monitor, 182, 183, 184–188

U

Ultrasonic alarm systems, 141, 142
Ultrasonic motion detectors, 143
Uplighting, 87
Utility power failure, 125

V

Vacation security, 32
Vandalism, 11
Vehicle protection, 167–176, 178

W

Wall-mounted lights, 78
Wall-receptacle GFI, 105–106
Warded locks, 51
Weapons, homeowner, 182
Wedge bolts, 51
Window(s)
  acrylic, 59–63
  basement, 58
  double-hung, 28, 54
  foil, 147, 151
  gates, 54
  glass blocks for, 63–64
  glass substitutes for, 59–63
  jalousie, 58
  locks, 13, 14, 28–30, 53, 54–58
  plexiglass, 61–63
  security, 29–30, 53–67
  shutters, 65–67
  sliding, 55–58
Winter storm protection, 139
Wireless alarms, 141